Technical Marketing Communication

Technical Marketing Communication

A Guide to Writing, Design, and Delivery

Emil B. Towner
Heidi L. Everett

BUSINESS EXPERT PRESS

Technical Marketing Communication: A Guide to Writing, Design, and Delivery

Copyright © Business Expert Press, LLC, 2016.

All rights reserved. No part of this publication may be reproduced, stored in a retrieval system, or transmitted in any form or by any means—electronic, mechanical, photocopy, recording, or any other except for brief quotations, not to exceed 250 words, without the prior permission of the publisher.

First published in 2016 by
Business Expert Press, LLC
222 East 46th Street, New York, NY 10017
www.businessexpertpress.com

ISBN-13: 978-1-63157-266-1 (paperback)
ISBN-13: 978-1-63157-267-8 (e-book)

Business Expert Press Corporate Communication Collection

Collection ISSN: 2156-8162 (print)
Collection ISSN: 2156-8170 (electronic)

Cover and interior design by S4Carlisle Publishing Service Ltd.
Chennai, India

First edition: 2016

10 9 8 7 6 5 4 3 2 1

Printed in the United States of America.

Abstract

This book is written to help professionals take action. Each chapter describes concepts and tips that apply to a variety of industries. In particular, this book is beneficial to the following readers:

- Marketing professionals promoting technical products and services will gain insight into technical communication and how to integrate complex information into promotional efforts.
- Managers working with writers and designers will learn terminology and principles that will help you evaluate marketing materials and provide detailed feedback.
- Technical communicators working on marketing projects will gain an understanding of principles and best practices you can integrate with your previous training.
- Entrepreneurs, nonprofit employees, and freelancers who want to develop marketing and promotional materials will gain tips and best practices that you can use immediately.

After reading this comprehensive, yet concise, guide, you will be equipped to engage in every aspect of technical marketing and promotion—including planning, writing, designing, and delivery.

Keywords

marketing, advertising, technical communication, promotion, copywriting, design

Contents

Preface

Advances in electronics, communication, engineering, and manufacturing require corporations and consumers to understand complex technological concepts in order to make purchasing decisions. Everything from toothpaste and disposable razors to security systems, banking compliance reporting, and farm irrigation are all examples of products and services that emphasize unique selling propositions based on technical features and processes.

The job of explaining those technical features and processes to buyers—whether they are corporate entities or individual consumers—falls on the shoulders of marketers and technical communicators. More and more, those two roles are being combined into a single technical marketer position. As a result, (1) today's marketers need to understand technical communication, (2) technical communicators need to understand marketing and advertising, and (3) both need to understand creative executions.

This book is designed to fulfill all three of those needs. It provides an overview of technology in society, technical communication, and marketing principles relevant to complex products and services in a variety of industries. It also breaks down the elements of effective creative executions, which will enable professionals to confidently participate in or oversee the copywriting and design stages. Finally, this book offers best practices for delivering creative executions.

After reading this comprehensive, yet concise, guide, professionals will be equipped to engage in every aspect of technical marketing and creative execution, regardless of whether their formal training is in marketing, technical communication, or neither.

PART I

Merging Technology and Marketing

CHAPTER 1

Technology and Communication

Before discussing the best practices of writing, designing, and delivering technical marketing, it is important to understand the:

- Role of technology in society
- Difference between technical communication and business or professional communication
- Overlap between technical communication and marketing
- Ethical perspectives relevant to technical marketing

Technology's Role in Society

Technology is all around us. But what does it really have to do with society? What role does it play? Although many people do not explore this question, they have strong opinions about it somewhere in their subconscious. Typically, those opinions can be summed up in two opposing perspectives: one that argues technology shapes society and the other that believes society shapes technology. Those perspectives are important because they influence how individuals feel about technology, even before they hear about a new technical product or service.

The idea that society shapes technology is known as the social construction theory of technology. Essentially, this theory argues that technology does not determine how humans act, but instead humans determine how technology is developed and used in different societies. An important aspect of this theory is how different social groups use the same technology for different purposes. For example, the open-source blog site WordPress was initially launched as a blogging platform; however, users discovered over time that it had broader application and benefit as a platform for website and e-magazine development. Cell phones have also undergone similar transformation and now serve as much more than a device on which to make phone calls. Cell phones now function as cameras, Global Positioning System (GPS) guides, hand-held gaming systems, libraries, flashlights, and more—depending on the social group and purpose.

The opposing perspective—known as technological determinism— argues that technology is not controlled by humans. Instead, this theory views technology as a force that changes the way people think and inter- act with each other. In other words, technology permeates society and dictates human behavior. Any change in technology is viewed as a pre- determined logical advancement, rather than a change in how humans view and use technology. Although technological determinism has been discounted by some, the idea that technology controls human actions is argued or implied in many articles, news stories, and social media posts about technology.

The bottom line is that some people view technology as positive and freeing, while others view it as negative and controlling. As philosopher Emmanuel Mesthene argued, "Technology has two faces: one that is full of promise, and one that can discourage and defeat us."[1] These two faces lurk beneath the surface of any discussions of technology; they influence how people think about the technology around them, frame technological changes, and read and respond to technical communication about the products and services marketed to them.

Key Concepts

Social construction: Humans shape technology and its uses.
Technological determinism: Technology dictates human behavior and interaction.

Defining Technical Communication

The term *technical communication* is not uncommon, but it is unclear. Some people simply equate the term with technical writing or product instructions, while other people are hard pressed to provide any defini-tion of the term. So before exploring the role of technical marketing, it is important to understand the broader topic of technical communication.

Most definitions of technical communication come down to two aspects: writing that communicates work or is associated with the work-place and writing that focuses on technology or a technical subject matter. In terms of the first aspect—writing for or in the workplace—the term *workplace* is often narrowly defined to emphasize organizational commu-nication. A number of technical communication scholars, however, have argued for a broader view of the workplace. Miami University professor Katherine Durack stated that technical communication extends beyond the confines of government and corporate workplaces. In so doing, she ar-gued that the concept of workplaces should include private settings such as household kitchens, where technical information about food prepara-tion is utilized daily, even though the work is performed without com-pensation.[2] In other words, work does not just mean work performed for pay or work performed for industry.

The second aspect of technical communication is described as writ-ing that relates to technology or a technical subject matter. Like the first aspect, this second part of the definition is often overly narrowed. For example, Durack explained how scholars and practitioners of technical communication often "conflate the term [technology] with computer technology." Instead, Durack argued, the term technology should in-clude knowledge, actions, and tools—such as "the knowledge of when and how to irrigate fields, and the entire set of human actions that com-prise this method of farming." That argument is similar to technical com-munication consultant and professor David Dobrin's discussion of the term technology:

> "Technology" is more than an array of tools and procedures. It extends to the way human beings deploy themselves in the use and production of material goods and services. One may speak profitably of an economic strategy or an administrative forma-tion as technology. The idea that by technology we mean a way that people, machines, concepts, and relationships are organized is crucial to the definition.[3]

Based on such definitions, this book claims that technical communication can be defined broadly as the communication of knowledge or actions related to tools, systems, and procedures. This definition can function like a checklist. When you come across a piece of communication, ask:

- Does it communicate knowledge or actions?
- Does it relate to tools, systems, or procedures?

These questions help us not only identify technical communication but also differentiate it from business or professional communication. For example, a letter of resignation would be considered a form of business or professional communication because it relates to the workplace; however, it would not be considered technical communication because it does not communicate knowledge or actions related to tools, systems, or procedures.

Differentiating Technical Marketing Communication

Now that technical communication has been distinguished from business or professional communication, two inevitable questions remain: Should marketing really be thought of as technical communication? Or is marketing just a form of business or professional communication?

Many technical communicators draw a distinction between marketing and technical communication. For example, Thea Teich, former president of Society for Technical Communication, distinguishes between the two by stating that the goal of marketing is to "sell something," while the goal of technical communications is to inform or "help customers use what they've already bought."[4]

In some cases, however, marketing materials attempt to move technology to potential users (or consumers) by informing them of new technological tools, attributes, and processes. Those situations should not be defined by the intent of the communication (such as, sell vs. inform), but instead should be considered both marketing and technical communication—also known as technical marketing communication. Technical communication professor Sandra Harner and marketing director Tom Zimmerman define this hybrid form of communication as "[t]echnology-oriented communication created and coordinated in a strategic fashion to accomplish an overall marketing goal."[5] This definition echoes technical communication scholar Carl Rohne's statement that "technical marketing communicators should be writers who are sensitive to the nuances of language...and who can sort a complex technical idea into marketable segments."[6] Taking the definition a step further, Harner and Zimmerman argue that one of the major roles of technical marketing communicators is to "create demand" for technology products and services by promoting features and benefits, price and value, and availability.

Key Concepts

Technical communication: Communicating knowledge or actions related to tools, systems, and procedures.

Technical marketing communication: Creating demand for technology products and services by promoting features and benefits that require the communication of knowledge or actions.

The definition of technical communication provided above can also help identify marketing material that should be classified as technical marketing communication. For example, when reflecting on a marketing campaign or promotion, ask the following questions:

- Does it communicate knowledge or actions?
- Does it relate to tools, systems, or procedures?

If the answer to both of those questions is yes, the promotional material would be considered technical marketing communication and, therefore, would require a combination of marketing and technical communication best practices.

Ethical Communication

Best practices related to marketing and technical communication are covered in detail throughout this book. One aspect that deserves mentioning upfront, however, is the concept of ethical communication in technical marketing. Technical marketing communicators can apply many of the same ethical principles that guide other professions. Those principles include:

- Rights—Concern for basic rights and welfare of others is at the forefront of ethical decisions.
- Justice—The costs and benefits of an action or policy are distributed among a group.
- Utilitarianism—The positive and negative impacts are considered to determine if the benefits outweigh the detriments. The ideal ethical action would provide the biggest benefit for the most people.
- Care—Caring for others is a prominent aspect of an ethical decision. This aspect considers the degrees of dependence and interdependence in relationships, the vulnerability of individuals and groups in relationship to another's choices, and the contextual details of situations in order to safeguard and promote the interests of all involved.
- Universalization—At the heart of this perspective is the belief that acts are universally right or wrong. To determine the ethics of an action, ask what would happen if it were repeated universally. If a detriment applies in all situations, the act would not be ethical in any situation.
- Common practice—This principle considers behavior to be ethical if it is commonly used in similar situations. Essentially, this principle assumes that common actions are expected by all parties and, therefore, would be appropriate. One word of caution here, though; this principle does not apply in all situations. As University of Minnesota communication professor Arthur Walzer states, taking existing practice as a standard risks leaving the impression that whatever is done and generally accepted is rhetorically effective and right.[7]

Notable Quote

"Real ethical dilemmas are complex and usually quite difficult to judge. Do not expect easy answers; in fact, be wary of them."[8]

—Paul Dombrowski,
Technical Communication Scholar

Although these principles are useful for general ethical dilemmas, technical marketing communicators must also consider what it means to disclose relevant information and provide explanations that address customer questions and concerns. This can be accomplished by using the ethical principle known as the Axis-of-Power Test.

Essentially, the Axis-of-Power Test assumes that people with more knowledge about a subject have an advantage over people with less information and, therefore, are in a position to take advantage of or mislead a consumer. This is particularly true when the subject involves complex technical concepts.

According to Georgia Institute of Technology Professor TyAnna Herrington,

> Those who have power to act or communicate information to others and are either obligated or choose to do so, also have responsibility to act and communicate honestly and completely without acting in a way that hides misdeeds or that misleads or masks information.[9]

Based on this, the Axis-of-Power Test calls for the technical communicator to put the audience on more equal footing in terms of information, even if that means the speaker must be more open or forthcoming to achieve that balance. This concept is unique because it must be applied to a specific context, is dependent on how much the audience knows, does not weigh benefits or detriments (although the balance of power is weighed), and does not consider common practices performed by others.

More importantly, the concept can be applied as a checklist to help determine if ethical communication is being distributed. Before delivering technical marketing materials to audiences, ask the following questions:

- Are you obligated to communicate about a technical product or service?
- Is the technical information accurate, clear, and complete?
- Have you ensured that information is not masked, hidden, or misleading?

By asking these and similar questions, technical marketing communicators can evaluate their moral obligations regarding the disclosure of information and achieve ethical communication.

Chapter Summary

This chapter has established a number of points that will guide the discussion of technical marketing communication:

- People often view technology as either positive (freeing) or as negative (controlling).
- The way in which people view technology influences how they frame technological changes as well as their interest in technical products and services.
- Technical communication can be defined as the communication of knowledge or actions related to tools, systems, and procedures.
- Technical marketing creates demand for products and services by explaining complex information and promoting technical features.
- The Axis-of-Power Test can help achieve ethical communication that is accurate, clear, and complete (without masking, misleading, or hiding relevant information).

With these concepts in mind, the next chapter will describe key marketing concepts that every technical marketer must understand and implement.

Recommended Resource

Readers interested in the history and evolution of technical marketing communication should consider reading the following book, which includes original articles from the early 1960s to the mid-1980s:

Marketing Technical Ideas and Products Successfully (Eds. Lois K. Moore and Daniel L. Plung. New York: IEEE P, 1985).

Endnotes

1. Mesthene, E. 2003. "The Social Impact of Technological Change." In *Philosophy of Technology: The Technological Condition,* eds. R.C. Scharff and V. Dusek. Malden, MA: Blackwell Publishing, p. 620.
2. Durack, K. 2004. "Gender, Technology, and the History of Technical Communication." In *Central Works in Technical Communication,* eds. J. Johnson-Eilola and S.A. Selber. New York, NY: Oxford UP, p. 41.
3. Dobrin, D. 2004. "What's Technical about Technical Writing." In *Central Works in Technical Communication,* eds. J. Johnson-Eilola and S.A. Selber. New York, NY: Oxford UP, pp. 118–119.
4. Teich, T. 2005. "Marketing Communication and Technical Communication: Not So Strange Bedfellows." *Intercom,* 52, no. 10, p. 9.
5. Harner, S., and T. Zimmerman. 2002. *Technical Marketing Communication.* New York, NY: Longman, p. 14.
6. Rohne, C. 1985. "Technical Communication in Marketing." In *Marketing Technical Ideas and Products Successfully,* eds. L.K. Moore and D.L. Plung. New York, NY: IEEE P, p. 234.
7. Walzer, A.E. 1989. "The Ethics of False Implicature in Technical and Professional Writing Courses." *Journal of Technical Writing and Communication,* 19, no. 2, pp. 149–160.
8. Dombrowski, P. 2000. *Ethics in Technical Communication.* Needham Heights, MA: Allyn and Bacon, pp. 7–8.
9. Herrington, T.A. 2003. *A Legal Primer for the Digital Age.* New York, NY: Pearson, p. 10.

CHAPTER 2

Marketing and Promotion

Although the term marketing tends to be used as if marketing is a single activity, marketing is actually multifaceted and complex. This chapter provides a brief overview of marketing concepts that shape technical marketing communication, including the:

- Differences between brand, product, relationship, and social marketing
- Four Ps of the product mix
- Methods for segmenting and targeting audiences
- Components of an effective marketing plan
- Legal concepts related to marketing

Types of Marketing

Not all marketing is the same. Some aspects of marketing promote products, while others build the company's identity. Before segmenting consumers or implementing a marketing plan, technical marketers must first identify what they are trying to accomplish and which type of marketing they should use. Although there are numerous types of marketing, this section focuses on four common types: brand marketing, product marketing, relationship marketing, and social marketing.

Brand Marketing

One of the most important duties of a marketer is to help establish and promote the company's brand. For many people, the brand *is* the company. A company logo is a visually recognizable part of a brand. For example, McDonald's has its golden arches. But a brand is more than that. The colors associated with a company are part of the brand. When you think about Coca-Cola, it is hard not to think about the company's vibrant red. But a brand is more than that. A tagline is part of the brand. Nike's "Just Do It" tagline still resonates around the world. But a brand is more than that.

The brand is what people feel when they visit a company's store, purchase its products and services, or even hear the company's name. It permeates a company's culture and undergirds every interaction people have with the company. In fact, a company's brand connects with everything from products and services to employment, financial performance, and even corporate crime.[1] Being socially responsible has become an important aspect of several company brands. Simply producing a quality product and providing friendly customer service is not enough to create a positive brand identity. Today's consumers want to know that the company focuses on social and environmental concerns that are in line with the values of its employees, customers, partners, investors, and especially the local communities in which it operates.[2]

In the end, a company's brand is developed and strengthened by its overall business practices and identity—from social responsibility and corporate logos to the prices, placement, and promotion of its products.

Product Marketing

The term *product marketing* actually refers to the entire process of developing and selling products, services, and ideas. This process is broken down into four aspects: product, price, placement, and promotion. These aspects are often referred to as the four Ps of marketing or as the marketing mix. Although the four Ps are intertwined, each plays an important role.

Product

As the term suggests, this aspect relates to the item or service for sale. It consists of features and benefits that make the product or service unique and desirable to consumers (when compared to other products or services offered by the company as well as the competition). Those features and benefits are initially considered during the concept phase and then are screened to see if they are in line with the company's goals and resources. From there, the product must be designed, tested, and manufactured. Finally, marketers must focus on product modifications and additional product lines that may relate to the product.

Marketing also involves the lifecycle of the product—ranging from the introduction and growth of a product to its maturity and saturation in the marketplace. In other words, marketers must focus on moments in time, since new features may be added or entire products discontinued over time while the product moves through the lifecycle process.

Price

The price of a product is the amount of money a company will accept for its product or service. The price is based not only on the cost to develop and manufacture a product, but also on demand and prices of similar products offered by the competition. Basing the price on the manufacturing costs is known as cost-based pricing, while basing the price on consumer interest is known as demand-based pricing. Of course, a third option would be to set the price based on the competition, which is known as competition-based pricing. The bottom line is that the price must be high enough to ensure the company covers its costs and makes a profit, yet it must be in line with the price that consumers are willing to pay based on demand and market expectations.

The price a company chooses is based on its pricing objectives— such as maximizing profits, recouping investment, or increasing market share. To achieve these objectives, marketers must decide on a pricing strategy. For example, a price may be set high initially and then lowered over time. This strategy is known as *price skimming strategy* and is often used when new technological products or services are introduced because it allows the company to recoup its investment faster and then lower the cost as other competitors enter the marketplace. One disadvantage of price skimming is that it may limit the number of consumers who are willing to purchase the new product (especially when a new type of product or service is introduced and widespread demand has not been established).

Other times, a price may be set lower than market demand. This strategy is known as *penetration pricing strategy* because it can result in higher market shares by appealing to a large consumer base. After demand has grown for the product, the company may raise the price at a designated time or slowly increase the price over time. When products or services involve multiple components, companies often use a form of penetration pricing in which the main component is offered at a lower price and the additional components are sold at a higher price. For example, technological products such as razors, printers, and even mobile phone apps are often sold below market value.

Once consumers have the main component, however, they must continue to purchase additional products or services to continue using it. Web.com provides a prime example. The company offers website and social media marketing services to small business. As part of its pricing strategy, the company will build free professional websites—including copy, images, and search engine optimization—for new customers. However, in order for the website to remain online, customers must enroll in a monthly plan to cover the hosting, updates, and traffic reports. The end result of this pricing strategy is that companies make more money from the add-ons or refills than from the main component. This strategy works because consumers feel they have already invested in the main component and do not want to lose that investment or take the time to reinvest in a different option.

Be careful not to confuse penetration pricing with *predatory pricing*. Although both involve low pricing, predatory pricing is intended to eliminate the competition by setting prices so low that both the company and its competitors would lose money if they continued to sell the product at that price. The idea is that the company will be able to temporarily absorb the losses, but its competitors will not. As a result, the competition will stop offering the product or may go out of business altogether. Predatory pricing is illegal or restricted in many places around the world, including the United States and the European Union.

Regardless of the pricing strategy that is chosen, marketers still make decisions about whether to use periodic discounts (such as off-season discounts), bundle pricing (such as discounts for purchasing two or more products), odd-number pricing (such as setting the price at an odd number just below an even dollar value), and so on. Some of those decisions will be based on company goals, while others may be influenced by the product's lifecycle.

Placement

Placement refers to the distribution of the product or service. In other words, marketers must consider how the product or service will get to the consumer. Some products are made directly available to consumers, while other products go through intermediaries (such as wholesalers or retailers) who buy the product and sell it to consumers for a profit. The benefit to the organization of going through an intermediary is that the intermediary already has resources and consumers in place to help expand the product reach quickly.

Generally speaking, three types of distribution strategies are often used by marketers:

- Intensive distribution—This strategy involves making the product available in large quantities and in a large number of locations. It is often used for impulse purchases or for everyday necessities (such as toothpaste, tape, gloves, candy, and health and beauty supplies).
- Selective distribution—This strategy involves limiting the number of locations where the product is available for purchase. It is often used for products that are widely used by consumers, but are more costly than impulse purchases (some examples include printers, televisions, dishwashers, lawnmowers, and chainsaws).
- Exclusive distribution—This strategy consists of making a product available at a select outlet (often only a single outlet within a certain region). It is often used for higher-price specialty items (such as automobiles, farm equipment, wedding dresses, and high-end jewelry or watches) that require sellers to have expert knowledge about the product and marketplace.

Choosing a strategy involves balancing numerous factors, including the uniqueness of the product, the price of the product, the target market, and even the speed and ease with which the product needs to be introduced to the marketplace. In addition, it is important to remember that the product's placement is intertwined with the rest of the marketing mix and can impact those other factors.

Promotion

Despite the frequent interchangeable use of the terms marketing and promotion, promotion is really only one area that marketing addresses. Technical marketing communication, then, could be considered a branch or type of promotion within the marketing mix.

Promotion consists of both paid and unpaid communication channels, including:

- Advertising—Newspapers, magazines, direct mail, billboards, television, radio, web banner ads, and so on.
- Promotional items—Coupons, product samples, gifts with purchase, logo items, in-store sampling, and so on.
- Social media and viral marketing—Corporate blogs, social networking sites (such as Facebook, Twitter, Instagram), online videos, text messages, Internet memes, and the like.
- Content marketing—Distributed information that is valuable and relevant to specific audiences, while also promoting a product or service. Although social media is often used to share the information, content can be distributed in a variety of ways, including newsletters, white papers, and even weekly radio segments.
- Sales and support—Inbound and outbound calling, sales representatives, customer service, technical support staff, and so on.
- Public relations—Sponsored events, news releases, articles, press conferences, trade shows, and so on.
- Word of mouth—Informal discussions about the product by ordinary consumers. Although this type of promotion is

driven by individual customer experiences with the brand, it is influenced by other forms of promotion (such as attention-getting television commercials or excellent customer service). As branding consultant Simon Mainwaring reminds companies, happy and well-informed employees can be your most vocal word-of-mouth advertising.[3]

Based on the wide variety of promotional channels that can be used, marketers must consider how each individual promotion relates to broader marketing campaign objectives. The need to focus on the bigger picture has led many marketers to discuss their promotions in terms of integrated marketing communication (IMC).

The main idea behind IMC is to send a consistent promotional message to consumers, regardless of which communication channels are used. In other words, whether a consumer reads a magazine ad, talks to a salesperson, watches a television commercial, or reads the product packaging in store, the consumer should walk away with the same consistent message. This concept has become more important in the age of electronic marketing, in which consumers interact with brands in a wide variety of ways.

Even though the specific definitions and applications of IMC often differ, the main takeaway is that marketing consists of multiple promotional activities taking place simultaneously and those activities must be coordinated in order to be effective.

Relationship Marketing

Relationship marketing shifts the focus away from products (and transactions) to consumers (and satisfaction). The goal is to establish long-term relationships with consumers that lead to a better understanding of customers, tailored promotional efforts, and ultimately repeat purchases. These customers, then, become lifelong brand ambassadors as well, providing that invaluable word-of-mouth marketing described in the previous section.

At the heart of relationship marketing is data. Marketers must know much more than customer demographics and psychographics; they must know each customer's purchase history, preferences, concerns, and so on.

Based on that data, companies can deliver tailored promotions that are not only personalized with each person's name, but provide information that is relevant to each individual. For example, the financial services company TIAA-CREF mailed out brochures to its investors, with each brochure personalized to display the investor's first name in the headline. More importantly, each brochure provided the investor with a simple personalized chart and customized text with statistics that indicated the recipient's current monthly savings percentage and expected monthly retirement income. The text was further tailored to feature additional subheads, paragraphs, and calls to action that related to the investor's unique situation.

The result of effective relationship marketing is that the connection between company and customer is strengthened. The company has a better understanding of who its customers are and how to meet each customer's needs, while customers feel that the company is treating them as unique individuals.

Social Marketing

Marketing principles can also be applied to broader goals and activities, such as social marketing. Social marketing should not be confused with social media marketing (which uses social media for promotional efforts) or with corporate social responsibility (which is the practice of aligning a company's business practices with the values of its stakeholders and communities). Instead, social marketing can be thought of as using marketing practices to achieve specific objectives related to social good.

If that sounds a little confusing, it may help to focus on the 1951 article by Research Psychologist and Professor Wiebe Gerhart that is often described as the beginning of the social marketing movement. In the article, Gerhart asks, "Why can't you sell brotherhood and rational thinking like you can sell soap?"[4] In other words, social marketing focuses on social issues (such healthy hand-washing practices during flu season), rather than a single product or service (such as a specific hand soap or sanitizer).

This concept is often used by nonprofit organizations and government agencies—especially those focused on public health or social values. For example, the American Legacy Foundation implemented its "Truth" campaign (www.thetruth.com) to stop the use of tobacco products. The campaign uses social marketing to promote health-related facts about smoking and chewing tobacco. Similarly, the Foundation for a Better Life implemented its "Values" campaign (www.values.com) to promote positive social values. The campaign uses everything from radio and television to movie theater ads and social media to inspire people to think about and model positive behaviors such as forgiveness, compromise, friendship, encouragement, and a number of other values.

The key point to remember is that social marketing focuses on social issues rather than products or services. Although that distinction limits its use, the concept is essential to those who are challenged with influencing social behaviors.

Segmenting and Targeting Audiences

Regardless of the type of marketing used, understanding exactly who the audience is and why that audience has been selected is crucial. To do this, marketers segment potential audiences into subsets. Although there are numerous strategies for segmenting audiences, some of the most common include demographic segmentation, psychographic segmentation, geographic segmentation, and behavioral segmentation.

Key Concepts

Demographic segmentation—Focuses on different facts about consumers, such as age, occupation, income, education, gender, and so on.

Psychographic segmentation—Often referred to as lifestyle segmentation because it focuses on consumer interests, activities, and beliefs.

Geographic segmentation—Divides consumers into subsets based on where they live. Those subsets can be based on a wide variety of factors ranging from counties, cities, and states to regions, nations, and continents.

Behavioral segmentation—Divides consumers into subsets based on consumer behavior. Some behavior factors that can be used include consumer knowledge of a product, past purchases, and level of readiness.

Once audiences have been segmented, marketers must identify the main (or target) audience. This can be achieved by considering a company's current customer variables (demographic, psychographic, geographic, and behavioral aspects), the competitors' target audiences, the company's objectives regarding market penetration or growth goals, and even secondary research about specific industries related to the product.

Based on audience segmentation and competitive analysis, the company can then narrow the list of attributes it will target when developing marketing. Although that list of attributes is helpful, most companies find it beneficial to combine those attributes into sample profiles that help marketers envision real people (rather than lists of vague attributes). For each profile, the organization includes a name, photo, narrative about how the person thinks and acts on a daily basis, as well as what the person wants to achieve when using the product. The key is to bring the profile to life so that marketing managers, writers, and designers feel as if they actually know the consumer on a personal level.

Notable Quote

"Visualize this person you're writing to . . . . She's a woman named Jill who's been thinking about getting a newer, smaller car. She's in an airport, bored, trying to get a Gummy Bear out of her back tooth, and reading Time *magazine."*[5]

—Luke Sullivan,
Award-Winning Copywriter

Marketing Plans

A marketing plan is the formal document that guides a company's marketing strategy by identifying its objectives, resources, and actions. Although marketing plans vary in length and content, effective plans have at least two things in common: they are strategic and specific.

Strategic

Being strategic means the plans are not based on guesses, whims, or hopes. They are based on verifiable data and agreed-upon objectives. That means incorporating the latest product data, financial details (including relevant costs and budgets), marketplace information (such as market share, competitive analysis, and pricing tolerances), consumer data, sales history and forecasts, and so on. This information will likely come from departments across the company, so successful marketers must establish relationships with people throughout the organization and ask for supporting documentation.

Specific

The more specific the marketing plan, the better chance for success. After all, the plan will be used to allocate resources, implement tactics, and evaluate effectiveness. Therefore, it must include measurable objectives as well as exactly what actions will be taken to achieve those objectives (including dates, budgets, and resources used). In the end, situations may change or new challenges may arise that require the company to adjust the marketing plan. That is part of business. The more specific the plan is, however, the more agile the company will be in taking strategic action that relates to clear objectives for success.

Marketing Plan Checklist

An effective marketing plan will include the following information:

- **Assessment of the situation.** This can include data about the current financial situation, strengths and weaknesses in relation to competitors, marketplace opportunities, target markets, and even upcoming product updates.
- **Objectives.** The objectives must be measurable to be useful. Simply stating that the company wants to increase brand awareness would not help in the future when the company tries to determine if its efforts have been successful. Whenever possible, focus on quantifiable objectives. What percentage of the market share is the company trying to achieve? How many units must be sold? What is the

continued

current level of brand awareness (statistically speaking) and what is the goal? In other words, think about success in different ways, define current levels of performance, and specify objectives to be reached.

- **Tactics.** Tactics refer to the actions the company will take. They can range from all aspects of the marketing mix. They may involve pricing strategies, new product lines, or changes in placement (distribution). Often, however, many of the tactics will involve the promotional side of marketing, such as billboard placement, earned and paid placement in magazines, web promotion, e-mail outreach, and so on. Once again, the strategies must be specific.
- **Budgets and timelines.** These aspects are inseparable from tactics. Once the tactics are determined, the next step is to determine how much will be spent on them and when they will be implemented.

Legal Considerations

Nearly everything a marketer does is regulated by federal laws, state laws, and guidelines that are intended to protect consumers and ensure fair business practices. State and local governments also regulate marketing and advertising through the state attorneys general and local district attorneys. Some of the most commonly applied legal principles include the following:

- Bait and switch advertising—It is illegal to use false statements or visuals that create a false impression about a product's quality, value, size, or use—especially when the false impression will be used to attract consumers and then intentionally switch them from the advertised product to another product of better quality. In other words, statements and visuals must create a true impression and promote the actual product that is being marketed.

- E-mail regulations—E-mail can be an effective marketing tool, but it is regulated under the CAN-SPAM Act. Despite the word SPAM in the name, the act covers any e-mail used to promote a product or service, not just bulk e-mail marketing. The act includes specific requirements regarding the e-mail's header (i.e., the "To," "From," and "Reply-To" fields), subject lines, identifying the e-mail as an ad, including the company's valid postal address, information on opting out of future e-mails, and honoring opt-out requests. Finally, even if a company uses an e-mail marketing service to send its e-mails, the company still may be liable for following the act.

- Phone marketing—The Federal Trade Commission (FTC) regulates the use of phone marketing under the Telemarketing Sales Rule. The rule consists of numerous requirements related to promotions, prizes, refunds, and more. It also includes the Do Not Call provisions. These provisions prohibit marketers from calling consumers who have registered their numbers in the national database. That said, the provisions do not cover phone calls made by charities, political parties, or companies that already have a relationship with the consumer. Phone surveys are also exempt from the provisions, as long as the call does not include any promotion or sales pitch information.

- Truth in advertising—Federal and state laws require advertising to be truthful, not misleading. In addition, when appropriate, the advertising must be supported by substantiated evidence. Although the laws apply to all advertising, claims related to health (such as drugs, alcohol, and dietary supplements), money, and high-tech products are under particular scrutiny.

- Child privacy—Companies that market to children under 13 years need to make sure they comply with the Children's Online Privacy Protection Act. Essentially, the rule requires company websites and online services to protect child privacy, to post a privacy statement that meets the rule's requirements, and to obtain parental consent before collecting personal information ranging from a child's name or photo to an instant messaging (IM) or chat identifier.

- Testimonials and endorsements—Although testimonials and endorsements can be effective, companies must make sure they follow the FTC's Guides Concerning the Use of Endorsements and Testimonials in Advertising. The guides provide advice regarding misleading statements, unrepresentative testimonials, lack of proof, disclosure statements that should be included with the testimonial, and more. The guides apply to traditional advertising as well as blogging and word-of-mouth marketing. Since these guides are not official regulations, failure to follow them will not actually result in penalties; however, it may result in the FTC investigating the company to see if any unfair or deceptive practices have been committed.

- Liability law—Companies are liable for products that are defective or harmful. Although many of those instances relate to design or manufacturing defects, liability also extends to the way in which a product is marketed. In other words, if inadequate safety warnings, instructions, or labeling lead to consumer harm, the company can be found liable—even if there are no actual defects in the product. Based on that, marketers must diligently warn consumers about hidden dangers and instruct consumers on how to safely use products.

Depending on the industry, technical marketers may need to comply with additional specialized marketing and advertising laws—especially concerning financial services, debt collection, tobacco and alcohol advertising, product packaging and labeling, pharmaceutical sales, and so on. Marketers always should seek the advice of legal counsel to help make sure they are following the laws that apply to both their industries and the types of marketing they implement.

In addition to the legal aspects described above, marketers must understand copyright and trademark laws:

- Copyright laws—Copyright laws establish who has the right to copy, distribute, display, or perform original works (or derivatives of those works). One of the most important aspects to understand is that a copyright does not need to be registered, but instead is automatically applied to any original work. In other words, once a person paints a picture or writes a poem, the person immediately owns the rights to that work. Another important aspect to understand is ownership. Copyright laws state that ownership belongs to the creator of an original work; however, ownership may be transferred if the work was created as a "work for hire" or was assigned to another person or entity. This means, for instance, that if a contract is not clear who owns a logo, then the creator (not the company using the logo) may own it. In addition, the copyright is not necessarily connected to the original work, which means that a DVD may be sold, but the creator still controls whether that DVD can be reproduced and distributed. That is because copyright laws apply to the expression of an idea, not the actual object (and uses are licensed, not sold). Finally, copyright laws allow for limited usage of original works without permission for the purpose of commentary (book reviews, educational lectures, and so on) and parody (which is different from satire). Overall, copyright laws are complex, and subtle differences can impact whether the laws apply. The best suggestion is to seek permission and consult legal counsel before using any original work (from images and text to music and lyrics).
- Trademark law—A trademark or service mark is any word, name, phrase, symbol, or device that is used to distinguish one company or product from another. Registering a trademark with the U.S. Patent and Trademark Office or Secretary of State provides greater protections. That said,

trademarks may be at risk of being eroded (or genericized) if misused. For instance, aspirin and shredded wheat are famous examples of product names that once distinguished a specific product but became so common that they were used as common names. To avoid such a fate, companies should make sure their trademarks are not used in a generic way. For example, when the Xerox trademark was at risk of becoming a generic name, the company began using the word Xerox as an adjective (such as a Xerox photocopy) rather than a verb (xeroxing). Band-Aid brand, Lego bricks, and Kleenex tissues are other successful examples of trademark protection. In addition to that strategy, companies should rely on legal counsel to aggressively enforce their trademark rights.

By understanding how to use original works in a legal manner, a marketer not only protects a company from expensive legal settlements, but also protects the company's own original works from unfair use or erosion.

Chapter Summary

This chapter described broad marketing concepts that technical marketing communicators must understand and be able to implement:

- Brand marketing is built on the company's overall business practices and identity—from its corporate logos to its customer service to its social responsibility.
- Product marketing consists of four main components: products, pricing, placement, and promotion.
- Relationship marketing shifts the focus away from products to consumer information and customer satisfaction in order to establish long-term relationships.
- Social marketing focuses on social issues (such as healthy hand-washing practices during flu season), rather than a single product or service (such as a specific hand soap).
- Potential audiences should be segmented into subsets that can be used to identify a target audience.

- A marketing plan is the formal document that guides a company's marketing by identifying specific objectives, resources, and actions.
- Consumers are protected by numerous federal laws, state laws, and guidelines related to bait and switch advertising, e-mail regulation, phone marketing, truth in advertising, child privacy, testimonials, and liability laws.
- Following copyright and trademark laws will help protect a company from expensive legal settlements as well as unfair use or erosion of its own original work.

The next chapter expands on these marketing concepts by describing technology's role in marketing and how to develop message frames when marketing technical products and services.

Endnotes

1. Fetscherin, M., and J.-C. Usunier. 2012. "Corporate Branding: An Interdisciplinary Literature Review." *European Journal of Marketing,* 46, no. 5, pp. 733–753.
2. Torres, A., T. Bijmolt, J. Tribó, and P. Verhoef. 2012. "Generating Global Brand Equity through Corporate Social Responsibility to Key Stakeholders." *International Journal of Research in Marketing,* 29, no. 1, pp. 13–24.
3. Mainwaring, S. 2011. *We First: How Brands and Consumers Use Social Media to Build a Better World.* New York, NY: Macmillan.
4. Wiebe, G. 1951. "Merchandising Commodities and Citizenship on Television." *Public Opinion Quarterly,* 15, no. 4, p. 679.
5. Sullivan, L. 2012. *Hey, Whipple, Squeeze This: The Classic Guide to Creating Great Ads.* Hoboken, NJ: John Wiley & Sons, p. 91.

CHAPTER 3

Technical Marketing

After focusing on technical communication and marketing principles in the previous two chapters, this chapter brings the two together. Specifically, this chapter describes the following:

- Technology's roles in marketing
- Framing messages in technical marketing
- Developing tests and creative briefs

Technology in Marketing

Technology is all around, especially in the marketing field. In fact, technology is integral to marketing in two key ways: as a resource and as a feature.

Technology as Resource

Companies use technology as resources for organizing, delivering, and optimizing their marketing efforts. For example, an article in *Harvard Business Review* listed seven marketing technologies that every company should use:[1]

- Analytics (tools include Google Analytics and Adobe Analytics)
- Conversion optimization (tools include Landing Page Grader and Ion Interactive)
- E-mail marketing (tools include MailChimp and Constant Contact)
- Search engine optimization (tools include Wordtracker and Google AdWords)

- Remarketing or customizing the online ads that a person sees based on the person's previous searches or page visits (tools include AdRoll and Perfect Audience)
- Mobile-ready websites that are responsive and adapt for optimal viewing to whichever device a consumer is accessing them from, including laptops, phones, and tablets
- Automation or technology that combines analytics, customization, e-mail marketing, and so on (tools include HubSpot and InfusionSoft).

Marketing technologies such as the ones described make up a large part of the marketing process, as well as budget. As technology continues to grow in terms of the number of resources available and expense associated with those resources, the need for Chief Marketing Technologists will continue to grow.

Technology as Feature

Technological facts and features are often included in promotional messages to help explain and differentiate products. For example, as far back as 1980, marketing professors Rolph Anderson and Marvin Jolson analyzed how technical features and attributes in advertisements influenced consumer perceptions of products. To conduct their study, they presented participants with three versions of a camera ad: a nontechnical ad, a partially technical ad, and a technical ad. Their research established that using technical terminology in marketing messages can, in fact, help companies differentiate their products.[2] That is just one reason why technical marketing communicators—like their technical writing counterparts—must be able to "identify and articulate the distinguishing technology characteristics" of complex products and services.[3]

Another reason why technical marketing communicators focus on technology in their marketing messages is to explain how a product works. The company American Outdoor Products provides an ideal example. The company manufactures and sells freeze-dried astronaut foods to the general public. Although the term freeze-dried may not be foreign, consumers may not quite understand what it is and how to reverse the process in order to eat the food. That confusion may make consumers hesitant to purchase the products. To address the concern, the product packaging includes simple explanations about the technology. For example, the Astronaut Ice Cream Sandwich package contains phrases such as "Freeze-drying is like suspended animation because it keeps the ice cream sandwich totally intact, but without the water" and "As you eat the sandwich, your mouth rehydrates the ice cream, restoring it to its original state." These explanations answer questions that consumers may have about how the technology works.

Before technology is integrated into marketing materials to explain how products work or to differentiate products from the competition, companies must consider how their marketing messages will be framed.

Framing Messages in Technical Marketing

As with every other aspect of marketing, message frames must be implemented strategically. In terms of messaging, frames "orient a reader or listener to examine a message with a certain disposition or inclination."[4] Marketing messages can be framed in a variety of ways, including customer-centered versus product-centered, focal and emotional integration, and agent–agency ratios. Technical marketers may also want to consider shifting to more technology-centered messaging as well as layering their messages to incorporate more than one method of framing.

Customer-Centered versus Product-Centered

The concepts of customer- and product-centered marketing are significant because these two strategies describe different methods for framing messages. In general, customer-centered marketing frames the message in terms of the customer's needs and benefits. For example, a hypothetical customer-centered headline for a golf club might read: Drive a Golf Ball 50 Yards Farther and Look Good Doing It. In contrast, product-centered ads frame the same message in terms of the product's facts and features: The Only Driver with Mach III Engineering. Understanding the difference between customer- and product-centered messages is especially important in technical marketing communication because the message can easily become overly technical and overwhelm the audience. By mocking up and testing these two message frames, technical marketers can make purposeful decisions about when to use a customer-centered approach and when to use a product-centered approach.

That said, technical marketers should understand the limitations of these two message frames. First, the frames operate on the basis that marketing is either focused on the customer or on the product—there is neither a gray area between the two, nor a third option. As a result, many companies struggle to develop and execute one consistent strategy. This problem is painfully obvious in Nissan's shift away from product-centered marketing in the mid-1990s because research showed that "consumers detest hearing about dual-side airbags and wishbone suspension."[5] After a little more than a year, however, slumping sales prompted Nissan to revert back to product-centered ads. Unfortunately, Nissan is not alone. Despite findings that companies can achieve success by implementing the same strategy over long periods of time, a number of prominent companies have switched strategies, including Dockers, Lincoln, and Woolrich. While some of the switches may have been warranted and ultimately successful, companies would be better prepared to make such decisions if they had a method for more thoroughly exploring and testing their options, rather than merely selecting between two contrasting strategies.

The second problem with pitting customer-centered marketing against product-centered marketing is that it leads to a narrow view of the topic, emphasizing only the *content* of technical marketing communication without considering how the product's role impacts the promotion. In reality, product-centered marketing not only focuses on product features, but it also positions the product as the main character in promotions. In contrast, customer-centered marketing positions the consumer as the main character with the product in a supporting role. In the end, these "main characters" influence how potential consumers view, remember, and position the product in their minds.

Based on these problems, it is clear that the question is not: Which is better—customer-centered or product-centered? But, instead: How can technical marketers expand and better understand the options available? The answer begins with the concepts of focal and emotional integration.

Focal and Emotional Integration

Advertising researchers Deborah MacInnis and Douglas Stayman introduced two concepts that reflected the different roles products may play
in advertising. The first concept—*focal integration of the product*—focuses
on what is being emphasized in a promotional piece. This concept is defined as "the extent to which the product is a central element" in marketing promotions. The second concept—*emotional integration*—deals with
the emotions that are depicted in a marketing piece after "use, non-use or
misuse of the product."[6]

These concepts and definitions are based on the belief that sometimes
a product will be the main element in a marketing promotion, and sometimes it will be a background element. Similarly, sometimes it is the cause
of emotions, and sometimes it has little to do with emotions. This is useful in two ways:

1. It moves messaging from *products versus customers* to *emphasis and emotions*.
2. It allows for varying degrees, instead of two opposite categories.

To better understand these concepts, consider two magazine advertisements: Nicoderm CQ and Prilosec OTC.

The Nicoderm CQ ad features a prominent picture of a woman looking into the camera, with her left shoulder exposed. On her shoulder,
the silhouette of the Nicoderm CQ patch is slightly visible; the words
"Nicoderm CQ" also appear in white letters over the top of the patch. At
the top of the ad, the headline reads: "Targets cravings. Helps you quit."
The bottom of the ad also features a one-inch banner with a few sentences
of descriptive body copy, as well as a picture of the product packaging.
In terms of product-centered versus customer-centered this ad focuses on
the product—Nicoderm CQ—and how it helps people quit smoking.
This is because the foreground of the image features the patch (the actual
woman is more of a background figure despite the prominence of the
image). In addition, the copy centers around what the product does—
that is, the product's role in quitting—with statements such as "A patented system that helps deliver a steady stream of nicotine to target your
cravings." In other words, the product is performing the action. Based on

that, the Nicoderm CQ ad can be described as high in focal integration because the product—both in its visual and textual emphasis—is central to the advertising message.

The opposite type of message can be seen in the Prilosec OTC ad. This ad features a mother and a daughter preparing food in a kitchen. Both women are pictured in mid-laugh; a variety of apples, cherries, eggs, baked pies, and dough cover the counter in front of them. Instead of a main headline, the ad features three lines of copy staggered over the picture. The copy features brief descriptions of events that take place on three different days—for example, "Day 2, happy day. The twins are home for the holidays." In this example, the consumer is central to the ad. Instead of the product or its features, this ad depicts emotions experienced by the consumer after using the product. The Prilosec OTC ad, then, is high in emotional integration.

Although the Nicoderm CQ and Prilosec OTC ads demonstrate two different messages, the products themselves do not determine which type of messaging should be used. Technical marketers must consider and test the options to choose the most effective message. One way to accomplish this task is to use these concepts to create a sliding scale of options by focusing on an agent–agency ratio.

Agent–Agency Ratios

This book introduces the concept of using agent–agency ratios to brainstorm and test possible message frames.[7] The agent–agency ratio is not as complicated as it sounds. Basically, the term *agent* stands for "who is doing the action," while the term *agency* stands for "what is being used." Using the Nicoderm CQ ad described above, the agent (or main character) would be the patch and the agency would be the patented Smart-Control system.

Technical marketers can use these two terms to brainstorm a sliding scale of message options. Creating the scale is as simple as creating a series of boxes that represent agent and agency options. To fill in an agent box, write the name of who is doing the action. Then, fill in an agency box by writing what the person would use. After one set of agent–agency boxes have been filled in, move left up the scale by turning the agent into the

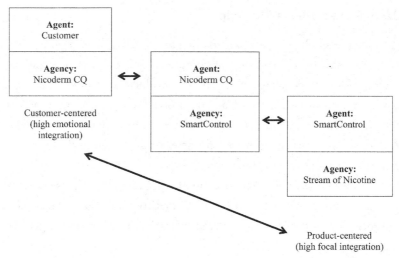

Figure 3.1 Sliding scale of agent–agency ratio options for Nicoderm CQ

agency or move right down the scale by turning the agency into the agent. For example, if Nicoderm CQ was the agent, it would become the agency in the box to the left. Conversely, if the SmartControl system was the agency, it would become the agent in the box to the right (see Figure 3.1).

As the Nicoderm CQ example demonstrates, the left side of the scale tends to be more customer-centered and higher in emotional integration. Based on that, emotional integration may be highest when the customer is the agent and the product is the agency. Any farther down the scale, the customer is not present in the agent–agency ratio because the scenario is too product centered.

Conversely, the right side of the scale tends to be more product-centered and higher in focal integration of the product. In other words, the further to the right that the scale extends, the more the message will focus on technological or scientific attributes and processes of a product's features (e.g., the process of delivering a "steady stream of nicotine" by the SmartControl patented system, as described in the Nicoderm CQ ad copy).

Thus, the sliding scale helps technical marketers move beyond customer- and product-centered messages to a third major category: technology-centered messages that help explain how a product works and, at the same time, differentiate the product from competing products.

Technology-Centered Marketing

Although technology-centered marketing may seem to lend itself to technically complex products (such as computers and cars), that is not the only use for it. In fact, large-scale complex products may move away from a technology-centered approach and opt instead to use customer-centered messages that are less complicated (and less threatening to consumers). Apple's iPhone marketing offers a prime example of a technical product that focuses more on consumers than on technology.

In practice, technology-centered marketing is commonly used to distinguish everyday products from their competitors. Take for instance Jafra Cosmetics' catalog copy that was used to market its moisturizing gel (see Figure 3.2).

Specifically, this catalog copy focused on "microencapsulated beads" that deliver "ceramides" to help the customer's skin "retain moisture." In this message, the microencapsulated beads were the agent, and the ceramides were the agency. Any farther to the left on the scale, the message would have been more product centered. This is just one example of a company that used a technology-centered message to differentiate an

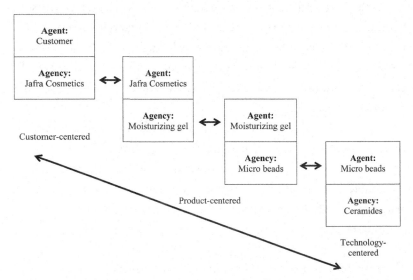

Figure 3.2 Consumer-, product-, and technology-centered options for Jafra Cosmetics

everyday product from its competition. Other examples can be found in the marketing of razors, batteries, watering hoses, shoes, and so on.

Although technical-centered messages can effectively differentiate products, they do not need to be used in isolation from other message frames. Instead, technical marketers may choose a layering technique.

Layering Messages

The layering technique incorporates two or more message frames into the same promotional piece. For example, the headline of a direct mail flyer for a Gillette Mach3 Turbo razor focuses on the customer getting a close, comfortable shave using the product. This headline is customer centered, since the customer (agent) uses the Mach3 Turbo razor (agency). Despite this message frame in the headline, the rest of the copy does not feature a single customer-centered message. It focuses instead on product-centered messages—Mach3 Turbo (agent) featuring an "Enhanced Indicator® Lubricating Strip" (agency), "Soft, Protective Microfins" (agency), and "Textured Elastomeric Grips" (agency)—as well as a technology-centered message—"Three Anti-Friction™ Blades" (agent) featuring a "patented coating" (agency).

By layering messages in this way, the flyer attracts the consumer's attention with a high focal integration headline, and then shifts to specific details in the body copy that differentiate the product in the eyes of consumers.

From Testing to Execution

Once a number of message frames have been brainstormed, they must be tested and, ultimately, described in creative briefs that will be used to create individual marketing materials.

Message Testing

To make sure that the most effective marketing strategies are developed and distributed, marketers seek the opinions of their target audience in the form of message testing. Marketing tests can be conducted at different stages, such as testing concepts early in the development process and testing creatives before finalizing marketing materials.

Key Concepts

Testing concepts—Early in the process, technical marketers can obtain consumer opinions about the products and features. This early testing is used to obtain feedback about concepts (such as message frames or key features to market) rather than creatives (such as specific headlines, images, layouts, or color schemes). By testing concepts, companies make sure their marketing efforts are on track before additional time and money are spent (and possibly wasted, if they turn out to be ineffective).

Testing creatives—Marketing copy and layouts undergo multiple steps before being finalized. This provides companies with the opportunity to receive feedback on headlines and images before money is spent on final production or even placement of the materials. Based on the feedback, marketers revise the creative to make it more effective before releasing it to a wider audience.

The testing of creatives can be conducted using a variety of methods. For example, a survey may be used to generate quantitative (i.e., numerical) findings about consumer preferences. Conversely, focus groups or interviews may be used for qualitative (i.e., narrative) findings that uncover how consumers feel about different aspects and why they feel that way. Finally, multiple methods can be used to generate a broad understanding based on both quantitative and qualitative findings; in other words, marketers are not limited to just one method.

Creative briefs provide the roadmap for turning broad marketing plans and research findings into creatives and campaigns. They can be used for marketing initiatives that are large in scope, such as a campaign launch of a new product. They can also be used for initiatives that are smaller in scope, such as offering an exclusive loyalty discount through e-mail or direct mail to consumers who have had a relationship with a company for five or more years.

Specifically, the creative brief serves three key functions. First, the creative brief provides an operational framework by outlining the objectives, strategies, and measurable goals of the initiative. Second, the creative brief helps ensure team members have the essential background information needed to develop effective creatives. Finally, the creative brief establishes clear direction, so all team members are working toward the same end result with consistent information.

Creative Brief Checklist

Include the following core categories in creative briefs:

- **Background information.** Include information on the company's brand, mission, or values if working with an outside agency. Explain why a product or service was created or updated. In other words, what market need does it fulfill? With promotions, include specific background on the immediate business need or longer-term business objective the promotion meets. Provide relevant supporting data.
- **Target audience.** Define audience segmentation (demographic, psychographic, geographic, or behavioral). Provide key information on each segment, such as their pain points, needs, or expectations.
- **Market competition.** Identify key competitors. These can be direct competitors who offer comparable products or services or indirect competitors who compete for consumers' time, attention, or resources. Outline the strengths, weaknesses, opportunities, and threats of these competitors specifically as they relate to the marketing initiative, product, or service.

continued

- **Goals and metrics.** Detail specific, measurable goals of the initiative. A goal might be to increase store or web traffic by a specific percent, achieve a specific sales dollar amount, or increase lead generation by a certain percent.
- **Compelling offer.** Outline the offer that will drive the results specified in the Goals section.
- **Call to action.** Identify specific actions the audience should take as a result of the marketing initiative. Should they call a number, visit a website and complete a form, post to social media, go to a store during a specific time, schedule an appointment, request additional information, and so on?
- **Functional specifications.** Provide a detailed workflow that identifies modes of delivery needed. For example, if offering an in-store coupon, define how the coupon will be distributed. This would then signal where specific ad buys would need to be made. In contrast, in an online promotion the workflow might identify a specific web page ad that triggers a consumer response. This ad would link to a landing page where consumers complete a form. Once the form is completed, the consumers would see a confirmation web page that directs them to check their e-mail. In their inbox, the consumers would receive a confirmation e-mail with a specific online code. The workflow outlined here signals the need for web ad placement and development of a landing page, confirmation page, and personalized e-mail. All of these require creative execution as well as web development.
- **Approval process.** Specify who must be involved in the review process, at what point they need to be involved, and who has final sign off. Do subject matter experts review accuracy of details? Is the marketing team responsible for messaging, tone, and look? Who resolves conflicting opinions and suggestions?

- **Timelines.** Based on the in-market date, the timeline should work backwards and include key sign-off points as well as time for concept development, creation, review, and revision. In addition, the timeline must include web development and testing, printing, mailing, and other production related to modes of delivery.
- **Budget.** Factor in production materials, postage, photography, media buys, in-house or outsourced fulfillment of writing, design, web development, and printing.

Chapter Summary

The chapter has completed Part 1 of this book by highlighting concepts used to develop marketing messages for technical products and services:

- Technology is used in marketing as resources for organizing, delivering, and optimizing marketing.
- Technology is also used in marketing facts and features that are included in promotional messages to help explain and differentiate products.
- Messages can be framed in a variety of ways, including customer-centered versus product-centered, focal and emotional integration, agent–agency ratios, and technology-centered marketing.
- Layering allows marketers to incorporate more than one message frame into marketing materials.
- Testing concepts and creatives allows marketers to incorporate target audience feedback before finalizing marketing materials.
- Creative briefs provide the roadmap for developing creatives and campaigns.

With the foundation provided in Part 1, the next section provides the heart of this book—that is, specific principles for writing and designing effective technical marketing communications.

Endnotes

1. Gudema, L. 2014, November. "7 marketing technologies every company must use." *Harvard Business Review*.
2. Anderson, R.E., and M.A. Jolson. 1985. "Technical Wording in Advertising: Implications for Market Segmentation." In *Marketing Technical Ideas and Products Successfully*, eds. L.K. Moore and D.L. Plung. New York, NY: IEEE P.
3. Harner, S.W., and T.G. Zimmerman. 2002. *Technical Marketing Communication*. New York, NY: Longman, p. 19.
4. Sussman, L. 1999, July–August. "How to Frame a Message: The Art of Persuasion and Negotiations." *Business Horizons*, p. 2.
5. Levine, J. 1996, December 16. "Brands with Feeling." *Forbes*, p. 293.
6. MacInnis, D.J., and D.M. Stayman. 1993. "Focal and Emotional Integration: Constructs, Measures, and Preliminary Evidence." *Journal of Advertising*, 22, no. 4, p. 52.
7. The terms *agent* and *agency* are part of Kenneth Burke's five terms of dramatism, as described in *A Grammar of Motives,* published in 1969 by University of California Press, Berkeley, CA.

PART II

Writing and Designing Technical Marketing Communication

CHAPTER 4

Working with Words

Few things ignite imagination like the words in marketing materials. They can evoke emotion, provide explanations, establish desire, connect with values, and provoke action. This chapter highlights the techniques that copywriters use to convey a company's message. Specifically, this chapter focuses on three Bs of copywriting:

- Big ideas (that shape marketing creatives)
- Beginnings and endings (that get results)
- Body copy basics (that every writer needs to know).

Big Ideas

Unique Selling Propositions

Consumers want to know what makes a product or service unique and why they should spend their money on it. To answer these questions, technical marketers need to establish a unique selling proposition (USP).

The USP may be based on two aspects. First, the USP can be based on a company's brand. For example, Dollar Shave Club portrays a brand of convenience. According to the company's marketing, men no longer need to travel to a store, find the right razor, have a store employee unlock the cabinet containing the replacement blades, and then pay high prices. Instead, Dollar Shave Club will ship an inexpensive razor right to the door. Not surprisingly, the company employs a USP that focuses on convenience—often focusing on the pain of purchasing competing products.

The second aspect that the USP may be based on is the product's feature(s). Take for example the Gillette Fusion ProGlide Manual razor and the Micro Touch One razor. Both products establish a USP based on the number of razor blades. The Fusion ProGlide Manual's USP is based on five blades that are marketed as thinner to provide maximum contact and a closer shave with less hair pulling. The Micro Touch One's USP, on the other hand, is based on having only one razor blade. According to this marketing approach, a single-blade razor is easier to clean and has credibility because one blade is the standard of professional barbers. In other words, both products are unique because of the number of blades they offer: one is unique because it has five blades, while the other is unique because it has one blade.

Regardless of whether the USP is based on the company brand or the product's feature(s), an effective USP either states (or strongly implies) the benefit to the consumer. After all, consumers do not just want to know how a product is different; they want to know what that difference will do for them.

Features Versus Benefits

No one really wants to purchase a feature. They do not buy the gel grip handle on Pilot's Dr. Grip Gel pen. They do not want the SportShift transmission offered by Acura. They do not even want the sharp-turning steering wheel available on Craftsman lawn mowers. Customers do, however, want the benefit that those features offer. They want a comfortable pen that reduces writing fatigue, and Pilot's Dr. Grip Gel pen delivers it. They want to accelerate quickly or control shifting on hills, and Acura's SportShift transmission provides it. They want to easily mow around (yet near) obstacles, and Craftsman's Tight Turn lawn mower provides it. In other words, customers do not really want features; they want benefits.

This benefit concept is important to understand in all marketing but especially when promoting technical products and services. That is because internal corporate communication about product differentiation typically focuses on technical aspects. The technical marketing copywriter's job is to turn those conversations around in the marketing material so that the benefits are prominent. That does not mean that features should never be mentioned. It just means that no feature should be mentioned in marketing materials without a benefit statement as well. Pilot's Dr. Grip Gel pen follows that rule by stating that its cushion grip (which is the feature) alleviates writing fatigue (which is the benefit). Better still, copywriters can make sure that a product's benefits are not overshadowed simply by flipping the feature-benefit order of a sentence and listing the benefit first. For example, copy for Pilot's Dr. Grip Gel pen could be written to state that it alleviates writing fatigue (benefit) with its cushion grip (feature).

Separating features from benefits sounds easy, and it is. Unfortunately, it is also easy to overlook these aspects when writing marketing materials—especially when speaking with the company's executives, engineers, and other product developers. That is because internal employees often refer to the features that they have created or worked on. So, naturally, when they discuss upcoming promotions or review marketing creatives, they will likely focus on the features.

To make sure that features and benefits are used effectively in technical marketing, just remember that features are nothing more than facts about a product. Therefore, feature statements can be thought of as focusing on the company or product. Benefits, on the other hand, focus on the end result of the fact and, as a result, place consumers in the spotlight (see Table 4.1).

Focusing on benefits can help technical marketers demonstrate that they understand their customers' problems, they offer solutions, and they put their customers first (see the "You" attitude section that follows for more on this topic).

Table 4.1 The difference between features and benefits in technical marketing

	Feature	Benefit
Definition	A fact about a product or service	A result of the fact
Example	Craftsman lawn mowers include Tight Turn technology	Easily mow around trees and flower beds in one pass without leaving any grass uncut
Main focus of the statement	Company or product	Customer

Dramatizing the Benefit

Including a benefit statement in technical marketing is not enough, however. The benefit has to be memorable. It has to be specific. It has to be larger than life. Technical marketers can dramatize the benefit by highlighting specific capabilities. For example, Craftsman does not just say that its mower can closely maneuver around obstacles; instead, it focuses on how it can mow around a small bird bath with one pass—and do so with a 50 percent tighter turn radius than the competition. In addition, technical marketers can highlight scenarios. Volkswagen's Beetle ad in the 1960s provides a perfect example. To dramatize the Beetle's ability to drive safely in winter conditions, the company ran the now-famous ad in which a snowplow driver uses a Beetle to get to and from work. The snowplow driver provides a dramatized situation because it focuses on a person who drives in extreme winter conditions. Customers are left with the impression that the car will meet their winter-driving needs, if it works for someone who drives in much more hazardous conditions.

The point is that technical marketers not only must make the benefit apparent to consumers; they must dramatize it in such a way that it embeds itself in consumers' minds. Not by trickery, faking, or overpromising the benefit, though (such as showing a car flying through the air, only to have the fine print state that cars cannot really fly).

In the end, the best way to dramatize the benefit is to simply consider scenarios that customers may find themselves in and then demonstrate how the product can help. If technical marketers do that, the benefit, features, and dramatization will all fall into place.

The Benefit of the Benefit

One way to develop scenarios to dramatize a benefit is to apply the *benefit of the benefit* concept. The benefit of the benefit is simply a way to brainstorm customer wants and needs that are related to a product (and its features). To circle back to the example mentioned above, the benefit of Craftsman's Tight Turn technology is that it allows customers to mow around trees and flower beds in one pass without leaving any grass uncut. But that statement can be taken a step further to consider the positive action that results from the benefit, such as reducing the need for the customer to circle objects multiple times or to follow up with additional trimming (see Table 4.2).

Extending product marketing to the benefit of the benefit enables technical marketers to develop creatives that highlight its consumers' wants and needs. Based on the Craftsman example, the technical marketer could develop creative concepts such as "stop spinning in circles" or "never use a trimmer again." A variety of scenarios, headlines, images, and body paragraphs could be developed based on these two concepts.

The benefit of the benefit concept can also be extended to multiple levels to generate even more marketing concepts and arrive at the customers' ultimate desire. For example, reducing the need to circle multiple times results in customers being able to mow in less time, which in turn helps customers spend more time enjoying their yards rather than taking care of their yards (see Table 4.3).

Table 4.2 Defining the benefit of the benefit

	Feature	Benefit	Benefit of the benefit
Definition	A fact about a product or service	A result of the fact; something that the feature provides	A positive aspect that results from the benefit
Example	Craftsman lawn mowers include Tight Turn technology	Mow around trees and flower beds in one pass without leaving any grass uncut	Reduce the need to circle objects multiple times or to follow up with additional trimming

Table 4.3 Demonstrating the benefit of the benefit

Feature	Benefit	Benefit of the benefit (level 1)	Benefit of the benefit (level 2)	Benefit of the benefit (level 3)
Craftsman lawn mowers include Tight Turn technology	Mow around trees and flower beds in one pass without leaving any grass uncut	Reduce the need to circle objects multiple times or to follow up with additional trimming	Finish mowing in less time	Spend more time enjoying your yard, instead of taking care of it

Each level in the benefit of the benefit table creates new options for relating to customers. Creative concepts can then be developed and tested. In the end, the company is able to produce more effective technical marketing communications, and consumers receive information that is directly related to real-life problems and desires.

Storytelling

Everybody loves a good story. In technical marketing communication, the right story will not only demonstrate a scenario that relates to the target audience, but also convey the benefit of the benefit in a memorable, even entertaining, way. The key characteristics of a story are that they involve the following:

- Change or conflict to which the audience can relate
- Characters who take action and are impacted by events
- Causality (that is, later events are the result of earlier action)
- Resolution or closure

To begin and end a story in the short amount of time that the audience will pay attention, technical marketers should focus on writing a minimal story. A minimal story is a pattern or structure that helps readers to identify a narrative. Gerald Prince, professor of languages and literature, describes the minimal story as having three components—a state of affairs, followed by an event, which then leads to a different state of affairs that is the inverse of the first.[1] A key characteristic of this three-part minimal story is that the first and third parts are static, while the second part of the story is where the action takes place. In other words, the minimal story pattern looks like this:

1. A state of affairs.
2. An action or event that causes change.
3. An inverse state of affairs.

Although this pattern is based on literature principles, it provides technical marketers with an effective model for developing technical marketing narratives. For example, consider this familiar customer-focused scenario used in laundry detergent television commercials for decades:

1. Situation = A child's favorite shirt has a stain.
2. Action/event = The parent uses the laundry detergent on the shirt.
3. Inverse situation = The child's shirt is clean as new.

A more technology-focused story for the same type of product may look like this:

1. Situation = A stained shirt is put in the washer.
2. Action/event = The detergent's patented micro-soap particles break apart the stain.
3. Inverse situation = The shirt is lifted from the washer stain free.

This minimal story model can be used for any technological product or service—with the customer, product, or product feature performing the action or event. Simply think of a situation, imagine the role the product would play in that situation, and highlight the resolution. Minimal stories can even consist of images that are developed into mockups for testing or concept presentations.

Regardless of whether technical marketers use words or images to develop mockups, the biggest benefit of a minimal story is that it dramatizes the benefit in a way that consumers can relate to and remember.

Audience Imaginations

Never forget that everything in a marketing campaign is aimed at another person—a person with thoughts and feelings about how the world works. That means the target audience already has some knowledge that can be applied to a marketing message.

For example, when people think of a rhinoceros, they see strength and size. Mitsubishi used these connotations to promote its Pajero sport utility vehicle (SUV) in a magazine ad. The ad hinged on a visual showing the SUV's body being suspended in the air, revealing a large rhinoceros where the chassis and frame should be. The ad's copy did not mention the rhinoceros at all. Instead, it simply stated that the Pajero delivered stability and control, even without the help of the driver. The rhinoceros image not only caught the reader's attention, but it helped Mitsubishi dramatize strength and the SUV's ability to practically think and maneuver itself. The entire message was completed in a matter of seconds, and it was completed in the reader's mind.

The key to igniting the audience's imagination is a concept called *closure*. This concept "makes it possible to communicate using implication. . . . When the viewer completes the image in his or her mind, it is often more memorable than a more explicit image."[2] To better understand the idea of how closure works, imagine that a marketing message is a circle:

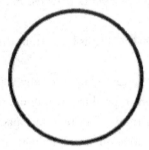

A marketing message that requires closure, however, may be thought of as a circle in which part of the line is missing. For the audience to complete the message, they must visualize (or imagine) the missing part of the circle:

In terms of technical marketing, closure strengthens a marketing message by asking the audience to be more active (rather than passive) in the message's construction. Think of it as a technical marketer throwing "a ball which then has to be caught. So the recipient is alert, with an active mind and a brain in gear."[3] In addition, allowing the audience to actively construct the message ignites the audience's imagination, thus making the idea more vivid and memorable.

CareerBuilder.com provides a prime example. The company ran a magazine ad that focused on an image of a woman, who presumably works at a clothing store. In the image, the woman is bending to her right to pick up a pile of clothes. Behind her, two naked mannequins are waiting to be dressed. The image is seemingly simple and may not even reveal its true message until after the audience reads the headline, which states: "Maybe it's time for a move." On second glance at the image, it is more obvious that one of the mannequins is in an action pose with its leg extended in a kicking motion. That kick is aimed directly at the backside of the woman bending to pick up the clothes. The reader is able to reflect on both the headline and the subtleties of the image to create a more powerful message about the woman's situation, thus making the idea more vivid and memorable.

That said, selecting metaphors, images, or clichés that will be understood by the audience and applied to the product's features or benefits is key; otherwise, the audience may be left with only a fragment of an idea that they cannot close:

Testing the concepts and creative mockups can help the company avoid such a fate.

In the end, closure may provide the basis for a new unique approach that dramatizes the benefit or describes a product or service in a unique way. All it requires is a little creative thinking on the part of the technical marketer. When developing creative concepts, ask what images can be used, what clichés or phrases can be given a new spin, or what metaphors can be relied on to convey the message. The technical marketer may also choose to describe only part of a narrative, allowing the audience to fill in the gap. In that case, technical marketers must consider how much can be removed and how much must be left in order to make sense. Be careful not to be creative for the sake of seeming clever. The goal is not to impress the audience with wit; the goal is to bring the benefit to life in a powerful, meaningful way that engages the audience. Finally, test the rough creatives to see how well they connect with the target audience or where additional tweaks need to be made to help the audience fill in the gap.

Beginnings and Ending

Headlines

Two elements stand out the most in marketing creatives: the visual and the headline. That means the headline is the most important written aspect of technical marketing communication. If the audience does not read it, they probably would not read the body copy or the call to action. The entire marketing message is on the line. So make every word count.

Specifically, a headline must achieve three over-riding goals, which we will refer to as the "Triple A Approach" to headlines.

Attention

Headlines gain attention. An intriguing image may make the reader pause but seldom will be able to sell products and services on their own. To help the headline gain the reader's attention, make them concise and specific.

Conciseness comes from revision. Sometimes it comes from cutting every word that is not absolutely necessary. Other times, two to three words may be replaced by one word that is more direct. Still, other times the entire headline may need to be inverted or cut in half. By cutting unnecessary words, the headline appears more approachable and less work to readers. It also has more room for specific details. That may be an important statistic (such as time or money savings). It may be promising a number of ways the product can help (such as "7 Ways to Balance Your Budget").

Audience

An effective headline will speak directly to the target audience. It shouts the words that the target audience would say themselves. It takes on a tone that the target audience can relate to personally. It also focuses on the benefit that matters most to the target audience.

Tailoring the headline entirely to one audience risks alienating others, however. That is ok. The goal is not to gain the attention of every person; the goal is to draw in the right type of person—the one identified in the marketing plan and creative brief. Focus on that person, on speaking to that person, on moving that person to action with a meaningful, memorable headline.

Answers

Once the headline has gained the attention of the target audience, it needs to provide answers. Sometimes it must explain what the main visual or metaphor means. Other times it needs to drive home the benefit in a memorable phrase. Every time, however, the headline needs to direct the audience to the rest of the copy.

Striking a balance with your headline can be difficult. On the one hand, the headline needs to be able to stand on its own and deliver a complete message about the product's benefit to a particular target audience. (After all, many consumers may only see the headline and then move on.) On the other hand, the headline needs to give the audience a reason to stay engaged with the marketing material.

Generally speaking, direct messages get the entire message across in the headline. For example, a flyer distributed by Stearns Electric Association in Minnesota included a headline that read: "Balance Your Bills with Budget Billing." The headline not only highlights a product feature (i.e., Budget Billing), but also states the benefit up front (i.e., balance your bills)—all in six words. Consumers who are concerned about balancing their budgets still have a reason to read the body copy in order to learn more about the benefit.

Incomplete or indirect messages are less likely to stand on their own but have stronger connections to the body copy. For example, the now-classic U.S. Music School ad from 1926 included a large headline that read: "They Laughed When I Sat Down at the Piano But When I started to Play!" The headline created a story that could only be finished by reading the body copy.

Five Headlines to Try

Copywriter Robert W. Bly compiled a long list of options that marketing writers should consider when writing a headline.[4] Here are five of those ideas that apply particularly well to technical marketing communication headlines:

- **New or unique words.** Conventional wisdom reminds writers to shy away from complex jargon, but sometimes those words can help the product stand apart from the competition—especially when developing technology-focused messages. Complex jargon can also be renamed to more accessible language that describes the technology, such as *viscoelastic polyurethane foam* which is now commonly referred to as *memory foam* and can be found in mattresses, pillows and shoes.
- **Statistics and numbers.** Learn everything about the product or service. Read the research. Talk to the product engineers. Read product reviews. And take notes about every number or statistic. Then, try every one of them in a headline. Most of them would not work, but the ones that do will be gems.
- **Objections and concerns.** What is stopping the customer from making a purchase? This question is particularly important when introducing a new type of product or technology. Whatever the answer is, consider addressing it head on. A headline can answer a question that has come up in focus group research, explain why an objection is unfounded, and ease concerns by highlighting what will really happen when they choose the product or service.
- **Comparisons.** Use the headline to compare the product to the competition. Write headline options that focus on a wide variety of attributes, such as cost, time, ease, ongoing maintenance, ease of use, technological features, and so

on. Find an advantage, and then find the words to make it memorable.

- **News stories.** Pay attention to the current events, politics, global news, and hot trends. If a story is in the news, it is already in the public's consciousness. The right headline can build on that and even help put seemingly complex or confusing products into perspective for consumers.

Calls to Action

If a headline is the beginning, the call to action is the conclusion. In this case, however, the conclusion is not really the end; it is a transition to the next step. The goal is to turn a consumer into a customer. That means moving them from the magazine ad, from the radio ad, from the billboard, or from the web page to purchase the product, view a demo, or sign up to receive more information.

Five Call-to-Action Options

Moving people to take action requires a strong call to action that is tailored to the specific situation and target audience. Consider using one of these five options to incite action:

- **Something for nothing.** People love getting something for nothing. That may be a free trial, a free gift with purchase, or a free upgrade. It can even be a free informational packet or white paper. Finally, it may be the free hardware, such as giving away a razor for free, knowing that consumers will need to purchase replacement blades to use the razor more than a couple of times. (Note: see the penetration pricing strategy described in this book for more information on this approach.)

continued

- **See for yourself.** Consumers can read marketing copy and look at images all day, but still not be ready to make a purchase. Perhaps they still have questions. Perhaps they are still a little skeptical. Whatever the reason, the call to action can help overcome it by allowing consumers the chance to see the product or service in action. Options include providing a live or recorded demonstration (perhaps even a video hosted on the company's website or social media), a free sample-size product to try, a money-back guarantee if they are not satisfied, or even the option to use the product for 30 days before buying.

- **Now or never.** People are often interested in a product or service, but tell themselves that they will order it later when they have more time. Unfortunately, they forget or lose the order form. Using a call to action with limited time or numbers can help spur action in those situations. For example, the call to action may provide a savings or free gift that would be available for only a short period of time. Other options include special offers for a specific number of orders or callers.

- **Assume the sale.** Remember not to beg or sound needy in the call to action. Instead, use command verbs (known as the imperative form), such as call today, order online, reserve your seat, register today, try it now, and so on. The negative form can also be used, such as don't wait, or don't miss out. Command verbs are not rude or bossy; they simply assume that the product is valuable and that consumers want to know how to obtain it.

- **Divide and conquer.** The product may have a set price, but that does not mean it needs to be paid in full at the time of purchase. Make it easy for consumers to purchase the product by testing different payment plans. After all, four payments of $19.99 may sound more doable to consumers than one big payment of $79.96.

For the call to action to be effective, it must be:

- Prominent—This does not mean the call to action has to be
  the largest or most dominating element. At a minimum, the
  target audience must be able to find it. The better option
  is for the call to action to stand out. For example, the call
  to action should be less prominent than the headline, but
  more prominent than the body copy. It should also appear
  at a logical place. For television and radio ads, the logical
  place would be near the end of the ad. For printed materials,
  a common location is the lower right corner. For online
  marketing, the location may vary, but design features (such as
  call-out boxes, pop up or banner ads, links, and so on) should
  be used. Descriptive subheads can also help make the call to
  action stand out.
- Specific—Specificity sells. That is true for headlines, for body
  copy, and for calls to action. Consumers want to know exactly
  what they can expect. That can include dollars saved, sale
  deadlines, number of products that will be delivered, or even
  personal information that will be required. For example, the
  insurance company The General offers consumers the ability
  to receive a quote without providing personal data, with a call
  to action that states: "Get an anonymous online quote now!"
- Believable—Consumers are savvy. If an offer sounds too
  good to be true, they would not believe it (and would not
  do what you ask). Direct marketing guru (and godfather of
  horror film gore) Herschell Gordon Lewis describes the rules
  of believable copywriting by focusing on, what he called,
  the "magic word" *verisimilitude*.[5] Verisimilitude essentially
  means the appearance of truth or seeming true. This concept
  does not just warn technical marketers about the dangers of
  overpromising or lying; it can also apply to statements that
  are accurate. In other words, if the offer sounds too good or
  unbelievable, it may be more beneficial to focus on a more
  believable aspect. For example, consumers may not believe
  that a product can save a company 70 percent, but they may

believe that it will save 45 to 70 percent. A minor tweak may improve the believability and, as a result, the response rate.

Making calls to action prominent, specific, and believable will strengthen the entire marketing creative by concluding with a powerful, memorable message and by giving the consumer clear direction on what to do next.

Body Copy Basics

Although the headline may grab the audience's attention, the body copy does the heavy lifting in technical marketing. Depending on the product and audience, the body copy must explain complex information, overcome audience objections, reiterate benefits, position the product as a *need* rather than a *want*, and convey all of that quickly and clearly. That is no small task. But the following concepts can help make it easier.

Ethos, Pathos, Logos

The terms *ethos*, *pathos*, and *logos* come from classical rhetoric, but they still play a key role in today's technical marketing. Essentially, the terms relate to the three types of persuasion:

- Ethos—Using persona and credibility to persuade a consumer
- Pathos—Evoking emotions in the audience
- Logos—Providing sound reasoning and supporting evidence.

Persuasive messages will include all three (even if one is more prominent than the others). For the sake of clarity, however, each aspect is examined individually in the following discussion.

Notable Quote

"Of the modes of persuasion . . . there are three kinds. The first kind depends on the personal character of the speaker; the second on putting the audience into a certain frame of mind; the third on the proof, or apparent proof, provided by the words of the speech itself."[6]

—Aristotle,
Ancient Greek Philosopher

Ethos

Ethos is woven into technical marketing communication by establishing credibility or a trusted persona. That can be accomplished by building a marketing message around a strong company brand or by including verbiage that helps instill trust in the product or company. If the consumer does not trust the product or company, nothing else matters. As award-winning copywriter Robert Bly states, "In addition to getting attention, explaining the product, and being persuasive, you must overcome the reader's distrust and get her to believe you."[7]

Testimonials, certifications, awards, and even product reviews can all be used to establish ethos. Deciding how many aspects to include or how central they should be to the marketing message should be based on the situation. If a company has a solid reputation with the target audience, those aspects may only need to be subtly included to help remind customers about the ethos that the company has already established. However, if the target audience is not familiar with or distrusts the company or product line, more attention must be devoted to elements that establish or re-establish credibility. The automotive company Chrysler provides an ideal example of the importance of reestablishing credibility with consumers.

In the 1980s, Chrysler was emerging from financial troubles when it was caught selling cars with falsified odometers. Specifically, the company had driven its cars while the odometers were disconnected, resulting in inaccurate mileage displayed in some of its "new" cars. Ultimately, the US government indicted the company for the fraudulent odometer incident. In response, Chrysler Chairman Lee Iacocca issued full-page ads, which apologized for the falsified odometers and explained that the company would be extending the warranty of cars that were driven (as well as replacing some customers' cars). The entire marketing campaign was aimed at rebuilding credibility and trust with consumers. That was accomplished by transferring some of Iacocca's credibility and goodwill to the company through his personal pledge that the problem would be resolved and would never be repeated. In the end, Chrysler's sales were not hurt by the odometer incident. Had the company not implemented a marketing campaign focused solely on rebuilding its ethos, the result might have been very different.

Pathos

Aristotle believed that persuasive messages can stir the emotions of the audience. The same is true for technical marketing. The old sales adage is: sell to the heart; reinforce with the head. In other words, customers are often guided by their emotions, their desires, and their likes and dislikes. They then seek out or focus on information (product features, limited-time offers, and so on) that reinforces their emotional desires.

Direct marketing guru Herschell Gordon Lewis argued that emotional messages will always outperform intellectual messages.[8] In doing so, he identified the most effective emotions to use in marketing:

- Fear—This is the most powerful emotion, according to Lewis. Home alarm systems, insurance, and car companies often use fear by showing reenactments or featuring testimonials of victims. The key to using fear, however, is making sure that consumers immediately understand that the product or company has a solution to the problem and that it can remove the fear (and replace it with peace of mind, happiness, control, and so on).

- Exclusivity—Exclusivity works particularly well on early adopters of new products and technology. In other words, if the target audience desires to be the first on his or her block to own a new product, marketing messages should appeal to that desire. The long customer lines awaiting the initial release of the iPad and iPhone are a prime example of the power of this emotion.

- Guilt—No one wants to feel inadequate or negligent. Guilt is a powerful, but perhaps less obvious, emotion in marketing messages. For example, the National Fatherhood Initiative markets its printed material and workshops by highlighting how absent or inattentive fathers lead to increased rates of crime, pregnancy, abuse, addiction, and obesity in children. By connecting those issues to fatherhood, the marketing messages subtly challenge the audience member to ask himself whether he is one of those fathers who may be hurting his children. Pharmacy products often use similar messages, such as portraying a woman with depression as an inattentive wife who is harming her marriage. The key is creating a scenario that forces consumers to wonder whether they are guilty of the same negative or harmful behavior. The mere presence of that question in the consumer's mind can lead to a sense of guilt.

- Greed—Greed is nothing more than an intense desire for something. Sometimes, it is a desire for something that others have. For example, a car commercial may create a sense of desire for a new car. Often, however, greed is tied to something people cannot touch, taste, or smell. It is tied to a feeling. Commercials show parents passing on the keys to the safe, reliable family car and obtaining the status of heroes in the process. Communication technology (from phones to video-conferencing) promotes human connection. The word FREE evokes the desire to obtain something for nothing. People long to be admired or validated by their family and friends, and marketing messages often promise to help consumers achieve that desire.

By focusing on emotional appeals, technical marketers are not only better able to understand their target audiences, but also to develop marketing creatives that demonstrate how technical products can help them achieve their desires (and avoid their worst fears). Always ask: How do consumers feel about the product or a problem situation that the product helps solve? Then, ask: How should consumers feel after seeing this marketing creative? If the creative does not achieve the result, rework the creative.

Logos

Aristotle's third persuasive element, logos, basically refers to the reasoning that is used to make a persuasive case, including deductive and inductive reasoning. In terms of technical marketing, logos simply focuses on how the marketing creative proves its claims. That proof may consist of facts, statistics, quotes, or examples. Deciding which elements to include depends on the product and the target audience. As Professor Leigh Henson of Missouri State University explained:

> Technically informed buyers, who already understand why they need or want the product, crave complete, accurate, and specific facts.... Less informed buyers need to be told about a product's benefits, and a copywriter's claims must be supported convincingly with facts.[9]

For the facts and information to be persuasive, they must be specific and relevant. For example, to persuade consumers, many businesses have begun integrating social proof into their marketing messages. Social proof is based on the idea that people are influenced by (and ultimately conform to) the behaviors and opinions of other people in society. Research studies have demonstrated the effectiveness of this approach in different types of industries. One study showed that nearly half of hotel guests are persuaded to reuse their towels when they find out that "75 percent of guests who stayed in this room reuse towels."[10] Compare that to less than one-third of hotel guests who were persuaded when asked to reuse towels to "help the environment." Another study found that homeowners are influenced more by messages about their neighbors' energy conservation than they are about saving money.[11]

Braiding Ethos, Pathos, and Logos into Messages

Although they are described as individual types of persuasion, the three types are often described as making up the rhetorical triangle. Perhaps a more accurate analogy would be a hair braid. Braiding begins by dividing the hair into three sections that are then woven together by repeatedly overlapping one after the other. After just a few overlaps, it is hard to tell which section is from the left side, which is from the middle, and which is from the right. The sections blend together to form a secure braid. The same is true for effective technical marketing; ethos, pathos, and logos must be woven together into a concise message that can withstand consumer skepticism.

Conciseness

Imagine a person walking on a trail through the woods. The well-worn trail is free of branches or stumps as it curves left and right down a relaxing path, which allows the walker to pay more attention to the sights and sounds of the woods—the squirrels running, birds chirping, and so on.

Suddenly, the walker comes across a portion of the trail where a tree has fallen across the path. The walker finds a way to climb over the fallen tree, only to find the trail progressively gets worse. More branches are strewn across the trail, and weeds and stumps overtake the path. The walker is confused and frustrated, wondering which way the overgrown trail goes or how to navigate the deadwood that clutters the walkway. Before long, the walker gives up, turns around, and vows never to walk the trail again. It is too frustrating. It is not worth the effort.

Now imagine the trail is not really a trail; it is an analogy for a marketing brochure, and the person walking is a consumer trying to decide whether to take the next step toward purchasing a product. The analogy of the trail is apt because consumers can easily become frustrated by confusing, unimaginative text that goes on and on with little focus or direction. The consumer gives up, drops the brochure, and vows never to consider the product again. It is too frustrating. It is not worth the effort.

The bottom line is that technical marketing communication must be complete, but it must also be concise. Those two qualities are not contradictory; they are complementary. Concise sentences make room for more details. The task before the technical marketer is to make sure the text is as easy to follow (even as enjoyable or as relaxing) as walking down a well-cleared trail through the woods. That means cutting out the deadwood, by removing unimaginative phrases (such as good or great) or complex jargon, and clearing unnecessary words or pieces of information that go off topic or lead to a dead end.

Yes, it can be a time-consuming work. It is a detail-oriented work. But it is the type of work that sets a professional technical marketer apart from the novices. It can also be the difference between gaining and losing a sale.

Conciseness Checklist

To achieve concise writing, look for ways to:

- **Cut unnecessary words.** For example:
  - *Modifiers*, such as "final outcome" or "perfectly clear"
  - *Expletives*, such as "It is clear that" or "There are"
  - *Wordy connectives*, such as "the way in which to" or "to such an extent that"
  - *Gobbledygook*, such as "Reimbursements to which consumers are entitled will be processed and issued promptly."
- **Avoid redundancies.** For example:

  Original text: "The report is available on the company website. It is 14 pages long. The report can be downloaded as a PDF or Word document."

  Revised text: "The 14-page report can be downloaded as a PDF or Word document from the company website."
- **Simplify words.** Short words add power and improve comprehension. For example:

Instead of:	Write:
utilize	use
discontinue	stop
initiate	begin
accumulate	gather

Clarity

Clarity is an important part of explaining a product's features and benefits. That is especially true with technical products and features that might confuse consumers. To make sure the message is clear, use the following:

- Chunking—Group similar topics or information together. This helps consumers find the information faster. For example, product specifications (such as height and weight) should be grouped together, while ordering information (such as phone numbers, acceptable forms of payment, shipping time, and so on) should be grouped. The key to chunking text is to think of each sentence or piece of information as having a tag that indicates the category. Height and weight would have the tag "product specifications." Shipping time and forms of payment would have the tag "order info." Those are not necessarily tags that would appear in the text; they are just a way for the technical marketer to break the information into pieces, logically group those pieces into chunks, and then decide the best way to organize those chunks. The number of tags that can be used by the writer are limitless but should be specific to the product as well as the target audience. For example, an audience may need to be told the different ways that a product can be used. Or, an audience may need to know how easy a product is to install.

- Color coding—Color coding can help technical marketers easily identify and rearrange chunks of text during the writing process. For example, product specs can be highlighted in red, while ordering information can be highlighted in yellow. The color-coded chunks can then be cut and pasted in different ways to see which is most effective.

- Descriptive subheads—Once the information is chunked, use subheads to break them up. That will allow audiences to quickly identify the topic of each chunk and decide if they want to read a chunk or move on to the next one. This only works if the subheads are concise and descriptive because consumers typically only skim the subheads, looking for keywords that they already have in mind.

- Short paragraphs—Big blocks of text are daunting and intimidating. Short blocks of text, on the other hand, are inviting. They allow the audience to take in one idea at a time—especially when extra white space is used between paragraphs. That does not mean long paragraphs should never be used. It just means that those times are rare (and, even when they are beneficial, they are still much shorter than the typical academic paragraph most people learned to write in school).

- Sentence variety—Long sentences are useful when transitioning between ideas or connecting multiple concepts. That said, they should be used sparingly; otherwise, the body copy risks losing the audience. Short sentences are different. They grab attention. They add emphasis. They imply action. But they also sound choppy when overused. The key to using both long and short sentences is moderation. In some places, subordination and coordination can be used to create longer sentences that still hold the audience's attention. In other places, a sentence fragment may be the best choice. Make purposeful choices, and mix it up.

- Transitions—Transitions function like signposts along a road; they not only help the audience understand where they are in the text, but they also help the audience find their way through the information. In addition, transitions provide coherence and help establish a relationship between ideas and information. (TIP: Try using the transitions that are suggested on the next page.)

- Concrete word choices—Do not rely on abstract words. Instead, select words with specific meanings. For example, the words "great conference" could mean "informative conference," "affordable conference," "entertaining conference," and so on. Similarly, the words saunter, strut, stroll, and meander would all be more descriptive and clear than the word walk.

- Parallel structure—Add both emphasis and clarity to body copy by using the same grammatical form of words, such as writing "Balance your checkbook quickly and accurately."

- Typographical cues—Use bullet lists, bold, italic, all caps, underlining, and so on to help make sure important points stand out and are easy to skim. Use them consistently and in moderation to aid the audience and not to overwhelm them.

Nine Transitions to Try

To add clarity to complex information, consider using the following types of transitions:

- **Enumeration transitions:** First, second, third, final
- **Addition transitions:** In addition, moreover, and, furthermore, similarly
- **Contrasting transitions:** In contrast, yet, however, nevertheless, instead, rather, still
- **Cause-Effect transitions:** Therefore, consequently (replace "for this reason")
- **Precision transitions:** To be exact, more specifically, in fact
- **Illustration transitions:** For example, for instance
- **Restatement transitions:** In short, briefly, in other words
- **Spatial transitions:** Here, there, higher up, under, below
- **Question transitions:** What does this mean for you? Why is that important?

Consistency

Consistent writing instills trust, avoids miscommunication, and conveys credibility. At times, it means using the same phrase in multiple documents; other times, it means using a tone consistent with the audience or situation. To achieve consistent writing, review the company's style guide and focus on common problem areas, such as:

- Spelling (do not write "St. Paul" in one place and "Saint Paul" in another)
- Key terms (define the terms, and then use them in the same way going forward)
- Names (do not write "Tight Turn technology" in one place and "Closer Turning technology" in another)
- Commonly confused words (e.g., allude vs. elude, everyday vs. every day, peak vs. peek)

- Gender bias (write sentences using the plural form to avoid choosing between *his* and *her*; for example, instead of "Each customer will receive his refund within 15 days" write "Customers will receive refunds within 15 days")
- Accurate punctuation and grammar (even when writing in e-mail and social media).

"You" Attitude

Technical marketing is more effective when it speaks to the audience about topics and actions they care about. That is because most consumers are focused on their own needs and desires.

To make sure the body copy emphasizes those needs and desires, successful writers focus on the "you" attitude. Often, that means writing sentences that include the word you (or an implied you). For example:

- *Ineffective:* We shipped the order this morning with a 3- to 5-day delivery.
- *Effective:* Your order shipped this morning, so you should receive it in 3 to 5 days.

Regardless of whether the sentence includes the word *you*, the main point is to write with the audience in mind. Instead of stating what the company has done or will do, ask: What does this mean for the audience? Then, revise the sentence accordingly.

Positive Language

Consumers tend to respond favorably to positive language more than they do to negative language. That does not mean that technical marketers never deliver bad news. It does, however, mean that technical marketers should strive to use positive language and perspectives when possible. For example:

- *Ineffective:* We do not answer phone calls after 4 p.m. on Fridays.

- *Effective:* You can speak with a live customer support person any time between 8 a.m. and 4 p.m., Monday through Friday.

Using positive language should not be confused with lying or omitting negative information. Technical marketing still must meet the ethical and legal guidelines described in the first two chapters of this book. The point is to avoid scaring or frustrating consumers by using sentences that are more negative or abrasive than necessary.

Rhythm

Technical marketing copy must still have an aesthetic quality that the audience wants to listen to or read. Skilled writers try different techniques to not only vary that cadence of sentences, but also to convey emotion and actions that reinforce the marketing message. Some of those techniques include:

- Antimetabole (repeating words or phrases in the reverse order)—This technique delivers a powerful statement because the audience is able to reflect on the significance of the second part as more meaningful by comparing it to the first part. For example: *Live to run. Run to live.*
- Anaphora (repeating the same word or phrase at the *beginning* of sentences)—This technique establishes a pattern that allows the audience to predict the next sentence and follow along with less effort. However, it can also be used to set up a surprise twist that will catch the audience's attention. For example, *Car shopping is frustrating. Car shopping is time consuming. Car shopping is overwhelming. But car shopping is about to change forever.*
- Epistrophe (repeating the same word or phrase at the *end* of sentences)—This technique emphasizes a key word or concept by repeating it in consecutive sentences. For example, *Driving to the store is a waste of time. Standing in line is a waste of time. Loading your car is a waste of time. In other words, the old way of shopping is a waste of time.*

- Epanorthosis (correcting a thought in mid-sentence)—This technique makes the body copy feel like a live performance. It is as if the audience is witnessing the technical marketing team talking through the ideas for the first time, which comes across as more authentic and even participatory. For example, *Today's customers want—no, they expect—to connect with your small business using social media.*
- Ellipsis (omitting one or more words)—This technique results in more concise sentences, while engaging the audience's minds by asking them to fill in the missing words. For example, *Parents want to control you; supervisors, boss you; we, free you.* (Note: The words "want to" are missing from the second and third parts of the sentence.)
- Alliteration (repeating the same sound or letter at the beginning of two or more words)—This technique adds a smooth flow while also emphasizing key words. For example: *Super Summer Sale.*

Optimizing for Electronic Marketing

When writing copy for websites, blogs, e-mails, and e-newsletters, technical marketers must consider *search engine optimization* (SEO) techniques that ultimately determine where a company's website or blog is ranked in Internet searches. Because consumers routinely click on the first few search results, organizations want to have top placement on the results list.

In the relatively short history of the Internet (as compared to centuries of print), SEO techniques have continually changed. In the early days, technical marketers could simply load keywords in the backend programming of a website—even if the keywords did not relate to the content of the website. Since then, however, search algorithms have become increasingly more sophisticated to identify keywords in the content of a site.

Organizations should have an acute understanding of the keywords that consumers use when searching for a particular product, service, or company. Those keywords, then, should be fully integrated into the design of a website. Specifically, the keywords should be incorporated into the site's meta-descriptions, first- and second-level headings (known as

H1 and H2), page titles, and even URLs. Some members of an organization might prefer edgy or fun titles, headings, and URLs; this approach might be appealing to loyal consumers who understand and know a company's naming conventions. However, prospective consumers (who are unfamiliar with an organization, product, or service) will search the Internet using common keywords, which means they may only find an organization if that organization has optimized its website with those keywords.

Incorporating keywords in copy also helps consumers find information on your website, in your e-mail, blog, or e-newsletter. People on the web usually fall into one of two categories: those who skim and scan pages looking for information and those who go right to a search box and type in keywords. If keywords have been used properly, finding information is easier for all consumers.

Search algorithms will continue to evolve based on the business practices of those who control the search engines as well as consumer preference. In April 2015, for example, Google rolled out new business practices for consumer searches completed on a mobile device. The change dictated that web pages that met specific criteria for responsive, mobile-friendly designs would earn higher ranking in search result lists. For now, keywords have played—and will likely continue to play—an important role in SEO.

When it comes to SEO—and marketing in general—the key takeaway is this: stay on top of search engine trends, changing technology, and consumer search habits and preferences.

Chapter Summary

The chapter has explained how to write effective technical marketing communication by:

- Using USPs to make a product or service stand out from the competition.
- Distinguishing between features and benefits (and dramatizing the benefit of the benefit).
- Incorporating storytelling and audience imagination into marketing creatives.
- Writing effective headlines and calls to action.

- Weaving credibility (ethos), emotion (pathos), and reasoning (logos) into marketing body copy.
- Revising sentences to improve the conciseness, clarity, and consistency of marketing messages.
- Using the "you attitude" and positive language to make sure technical marketing communication is more relevant and effective.
- Improving the aesthetic quality of marketing creative with rhetorical techniques.
- Optimizing for electronic marketing, such as websites, blogs, and e-newsletters.

The next chapter explains how design principles can help convey—and even strengthen—technical marketing messages.

Recommended Resources

Readers interested in writing vivid, precise, and concise copy may find the following books helpful:

- *The Describer's Dictionary* (David Grambs. New York: W.W. Norton & Co., 1995), which suggests precise terms that can be used to describe everything from sizes, structures, and colors to the human features, voices, and attire.
- *Book of English Usage* (The American Heritage. Boston: Houghton Mifflin Co., 1996), which covers word choices-related grammar, style, and tone as well as gender, names, and scientific terms.
- *Edit Yourself* (Bruce Ross-Larson. New York: W.W. Norton & Co., 1996), which provides before-and-after editing examples related to conciseness, parallel construction, sentence order, and more.

Endnotes

1. Prince, G. 1974. *A Grammar of Stories*. The Hague, Netherland: Mouton.

2. Stewart, M. 2002. *Launching the Imagination*. New York, NY: McGraw-Hill Companies, p. 3.6.

3. McAlhone, B., and D. Stuart. 1996. *A Smile in the Mind: Witty Thinking in Graphic Design*. London, UK: Phaidon Incorporated Limited, p. 19.

4. Bly, R.W. 2007. *The Copywriter's Handbook: A Step-By-Step Guide to Writing Copy That Sells*. New York, NY: Macmillan.

5. Lewis, H.G. 1984. *Direct Mail Copy That Sells!* Englewood Cliffs, NJ: Prentice-Hall.

6. Aristotle. 1984. *The Rhetoric and the Poetics of Aristotle*. W.R. Roberts and I. Bywater, Trans. New York, NY: The Modern Library, pp. 24–25.

7. Bly, R.W. 2007. *The Copywriter's Handbook: A Step-By-Step Guide to Writing Copy That Sells*. New York, NY: Macmillan, p. 116.

8. Lewis, H.G. 1984. *Direct Mail Copy That Sells!* Englewood Cliffs, NJ: Prentice-Hall.

9. Henson, L. 1996. "Why and How to Advance Technical Copywriting." *Journal of Technical Writing and Communication*, 26, no. 2, p. 201.

10. Goldstein, N.J., R.B. Cialdini, and V. Griskevicius. 2008. "A Room with a Viewpoint: Using Social Norms to Motivate Environmental Conservation in Hotels." *Journal of Consumer Research*, 35, no. 3, pp. 472–482.

11. Cialdini, R., and W. Schultz. 2004. "Understanding and Motivating Energy Conservation via Social Norms." Menlo Park, CA: William and Flora Hewlett Foundation.

CHAPTER 5

Working with Design

Design is not art. It may rely on art techniques and principles, but design is aimed at communicating by helping people find, understand, and remember information. This chapter highlights concepts that can be used to visually convey technical marketing messages. Specifically, this chapter focuses on:

- Guiding principles
- Page design
- Graphics and colors
- Fonts and formatting text

Guiding Principles

Design is about more than merely placing words and images in a layout. Technical marketers must understand how the design impacts the audience's perceptions not only of the information they view, but also of the organization distributing that information. The following sections describe two principles at work in every design: presence and Gestalt psychology.

Presence

An important aspect of both design and persuasion is the selection of material. That is where the concept of *presence* comes in. In general, presence is achieved by selecting and highlighting specific elements in such a way that those elements (rather than other, less favorable elements) stand out. To paraphrase philosophers Chaim Perelman and L. Olbrechts-Tyteca, presence is essential to technical marketing because it orients the minds of the audience, makes one interpretation more prevalent, and provides specific elements with the significance they deserve.[1]

Since technical marketing is based on how the audience perceives information, it is important to understand the concept of presence and how it works. In his book *Figure, Ground, and Presence*, Robert Tucker explains three conclusions about presence[2]:

- A person can only interpret a figure in one way at a time. Take, for example, the popular black-and-white image that can be viewed either as a white candlestick (surrounded by black shading) or as two black silhouettes staring into each other (yet separated by the white between them). Although the image may be interpreted in two ways, the human mind can only consciously consider one interpretation at a time. In other words, the simple act of interpreting one element hinders the other element(s) from emerging or being interpreted.
- A person may switch from one interpretation to another. Although some interpretations may be easier to see, the human mind has the ability to toggle between the different interpretations. Therefore, people have some control over what they see.
- A person may be encouraged to interpret a particular figure or to switch between interpretations. In other words, by making certain aspects more prevalent or vivid (either through language or design principles), technical marketing can influence the way in which the audience interprets a message.

Based on that, technical marketers must not only choose which ideas and images on which to focus, but also must present them in a way that draws audience's attention to elements that support the marketing message. Although copy and concept can help focus the audience's attention, the design and layout of technical marketing communication play key roles in establishing presence.

Notable Quote

"What is present for us is foremost in our minds and important to us. Curiously, what loses in importance becomes abstract, almost nonexistent."[3]

—Chaim Perelman,
Prominent Argumentation Theorist

The concept of presence is even more important to technical marketers because it helps spur people to action—especially if the goal is to persuade consumers to try new technology or switch to a different product. That is because people cannot move from one position (or opinion) to another without a reason. To abandon the status quo, they must understand: why they want to leave *and* how likely it is that they will arrive at or be satisfied by the new position.[4]

For example, if consumers currently use a specific detergent to wash clothes, they would not likely switch to a new detergent without first understanding why they should try something new and, second, how likely it is that the new detergent will meet their needs. By endowing the new detergent with presence, the technical marketer establishes the status quo (or the old detergent) as so inadequate that the audience not only recognizes the reasoning behind changing detergents, but also feels compelled to act upon it.

The bottom line is that technical marketing must create marketing messages that persuade audiences that their current situations, products, or actions do not meet their needs. The concepts described in this chapter provide various approaches that technical marketers can use to make sure their products, features, and benefits achieve presence in such a way that they overcome potential doubts or competing ideas that consumers may have.

Gestalt Psychology

Technical marketers who design—or who critique design—should understand how perception, learning, and memory affect how consumers engage with content in a particular design layout. To gain that understanding, technical marketers can seek guidance from Gestalt psychology. In German, the term *gestalt* has two meanings[5]:

- The connotation of "shape" or "form" as a property of things
- A concrete individual and characteristic entity, existing as something detached and having a shape or form as one of its attributes.

The principles of Gestalt psychology, then, outline how people perceive shape or form as part of a whole group or as individual entities. As Gestalt Psychologist Wolfgang Köhler explained, "In most visual fields the contents of certain areas 'belong together.'"[6] He argued that objects do not exist as individual units without previous knowledge about "their practical behaviors." That previous knowledge influences memory and familiarity with an object and its use.

Imagine for a moment walking into a conference room. You might know it is a conference room because door signage identifies the room that way or you booked the room for a team meeting. When you walk into the room, you see the room as a whole; that is, it is a conference room. Individual units will begin to emerge with clarity from the background of the conference room, and you will begin to perceive them based on tasks you need to accomplish and your prior experiences. For example, if you are a presenter, you might identify familiar objects that you need such as a laptop station, a podium, a projector, or screen. If you are a participant, you might identify the conference table and chairs then identify where the presenter will be so that you can choose the best chair to meet your needs.

How do these perceptions relate to design? In the context of a web page, for example, a consumer might recognize a web page as a whole unit because it is accessed via the Internet, has a URL, and displays a general shape or form that is consistent with other web pages. Identifying the parts of the web page relies on a consumer's ability to perceive individual shapes and forms. Depending on the consumer's previous web experiences, a navigation menu, search field, or particular menu tab may come into focus. The design and organization of the web page (its layout) can aid—or impede—the consumer's ability to sense and distinguish individual parts from the whole based on Gestalt design principles. When effectively used in design, these principles focus and guide consumers' attention as well as help consumers achieve a task.

Page Design

One of the most important tasks a technical marketer faces is placing elements on a page (or screen). Effective page design attracts attention and provides structure. This section explains the most commonly cited Gestalt design principles: contrast, emphasis, repetition, alignment, proximity, balance, and flow. These principles serve as typographical cueing techniques that guide consumers and make it easier for them to engage with content.

Contrast and Emphasis

Contrast and emphasis serve several purposes. First, they can provide a clear focal point and entry point into a design. Contrast and emphasis also help guide consumers through a hierarchy of information in a design. Finally, they help consumers interpret overall structure and organization. While a wall of text might provide a clear entry point (e.g., the top left corner of the page), it does not entice a consumer to read the content because it does not provide inviting, manageable chunks of information. Likewise, a design cluttered with highly contrasted elements that compete for the consumer's attention results in no clear focal point or starting place.

Key Concepts

Contrast: Having qualities that are noticeably different from others.
Emphasis: Prominence given to something to indicate importance.

Contrast and emphasis can be achieved through varying the sizes, colors, styles, and shapes of text and graphics as well as the contrast of text on a background. While headings and subheadings can be used to draw attention to important information, contrast and emphasis can be achieved by designing these to be larger, bolder, in a specific color, set off in a contrasting color bar, or accompanied by a graphic element.

Placement of key information or graphics also allows for contrast and emphasis. In traditional print newspaper speak, for example, key information is often located "above the fold" where it is emphasized through prominent placement when newspapers are folded and stacked on top of each other. Web page design tends to follow suit with key information emphasized at the top. In direct mail letters, on the other hand, key information or calls to action are often set apart in the P.S. at the end.

Finally, the use of color can be used to create contrast and emphasis and guide consumers. Color coding can be used to identify and group specific content areas. A splash of color can also be used to create a focal point. The examples in Figure 5.1 demonstrate the impact of contrast and emphasis.

The example on the left in Figure 5.1 shows minimal use of contrast and emphasis. In fact, the only element that stands out is the main heading because it is larger and centered. The example on the right, on the other hand, shows how the simple use of contrast and emphasis draws attention to important information and provides visual cues to help guide the reader through individual chunks of content. In this example font size and style as well as color blocking and a graphic create contrast and

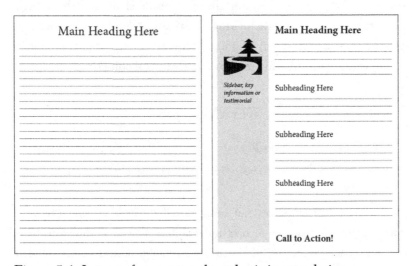

Figure 5.1 Impact of contrast and emphasis in copy design

emphasis. While the design is not award winning, it achieves its purpose effectively.

Contrast and emphasis are the most cited Gestalt principles in design instruction probably because of the key role they play. Contrast and emphasis invite consumers into a design and make it easy for them to engage with the content.

Repetition and Consistency

Repetition and consistency provide consumers with a navigational framework they are familiar with or can easily learn and follow. These principles serve two primary functions. First, repetition and consistency instill confidence in consumers by establishing familiarity with a brand in a particular medium. Second, repetition and consistency allow for predictability and scanning of information.

Key Concepts

Repetition: The act of repeating something, so it becomes memorable and familiar.

Consistency: Conformity in the application of something for the sake of logic and accuracy.

The following story illustrates the confusion that can set in when repetition and consistency are not adhered to. Comedian Mitch Hedberg was known for dissecting marketing campaigns in a humorous way. In one stand-up routine, he questioned the meaning behind the often-used phrase: "Available at participating McDonald's."[7] He joked that he wanted to open his own McDonald's—complete with the golden arches and everything customers associate with the restaurant—but he did not want to participate in anything. Instead, when customers tried to order a Happy Meal or Big Mac, he would say his McDonald's only sold spaghetti—and blankets. While this story speaks to the importance of a consistent in-store brand experience that is familiar and meets consumer expectations, the same holds true for repetition and consistency in design, whether in print, wayfinding signage, or online communication.

Tips for Repetition and Consistency

- **Reading patterns:** Maintain a familiar organizational structure based on typical reading patterns (top to bottom, left to right, and so on).
- **Branding:** Use colors, fonts, and graphics that are consistent with a company's brand. Include the company logo whenever contact information is provided.
- **Conventions:** Adhere to consumer expectations and conventions, such as the following suggestions for websites:
  - Provide navigation menus located near the top of the web page.
  - Include a "spyglass" icon or similar image to indicate a search function.
  - Provide a clickable company logo in a header of the page that returns the reader to the main home page.

Reading Patterns

While everyone's information skimming and scanning techniques are subject to individual nuance, in general, western world initial reading patterns tend to fall in one of two categories: F Pattern or Z Pattern. These reading patterns offer predictable hot spots where consumers' eyes will go and hover. Effective design will place key information in these hot spots.

The F Pattern is typical for designs that are text heavy. Consumers will scan a vertical line down the left side of the text looking for keywords or phrases. Once found, consumers begin reading horizontally. Understanding this reading behavior is important for content development and design because it reinforces consumers do not read word-for-word. Instead, they scan in a predictable pattern for keywords or phrases. That means paragraphs, subheads, and bullet points should begin with the most important keywords and phrases, and the most important information should be at the top of the F.

Z Pattern scanning occurs on pages that are not text heavy. Consumers typically will scan the top of the page, dart down and left, and repeat a horizontal search on a lower section of the page. A typical web layout that capitalizes on this reading pattern will start with a logo at the point of entry in the upper left-hand corner followed by a top navigational menu. A series of horizontal icons, text fields, or images will draw consumers lower on the page and lead them to a call to action on the right-hand side.

Consumers may not be consciously aware of these two reading patterns. Designers should be, though, and should ensure consistency and repetition in layouts that take full advantage of identified hot spots.

Grids

Grids are structural frameworks that provide harmony in a design family. How? Through consistency and repetition in design layout across all of an organization's brochures, web pages, direct mail pieces, posters, print, and electronic ads—everything, really. Grids are portrait or landscape in nature and have either an even or odd number of columns to divide up for content placement. Within this framework, there is a place for everything, and everything should have a consistent place: contact information, calls to action, bulleted lists, graphics, icons, corporate information, and so on. The examples in Figure 5.2 show how a standard, portrait four-column grid can be divided for a variety of print applications, including a newsletter, flyer, and sell sheet:

Grids yield efficiency in design because designers do not need to re-invent a layout with each project. Grids also provide efficiency for consumers because information is presented in a familiar and predictable way. That is, consumers know where to go to find what they need.

Figure 5.2 Relationship of grids to other print applications

Consistent, repetitive use of design grids can be likened to a consistent, repetitive floor plan in grocery stores. Consumers needing to buy a specific item—such as a gallon of milk—can walk into a grocery store and quickly orient themselves to the location of the dairy case, which is usually with other staple items at the back of the store because grocers do not want consumers to stop in for just one item. Consumers who are making a full grocery run will find consistency and repetition in the overall store layout. Floral, bakery, and produce are usually up front where the colors and smells are warm and inviting. Cold items usually line the perimeter of the store. Dry goods are stacked in the middle. Great deals and seasonal products are situated on end caps, and cashiers are the gateway to the parking lot. Just as consumers expect consistency and repetition in a grocery store layout to make their shopping experience easier, they expect consistency and repetition in marketing materials.

The grid concept can be applied to any marketing piece simply by dividing the layout using imaginary horizontal and vertical gridlines. For instance, a postcard layout may look like the one in Figure 5.3.

In the example in Figure 5.3, notice how the black box begins on the same vertical line where the headline ends. In addition, both the body

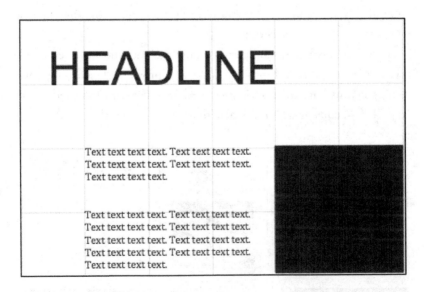

Figure 5.3 Sample postcard layout using gridlines to align and balance elements

copy and the black box begin on the same horizontal line. Finally, the left margin for the body copy aligns with the vertical line that extends down from the left edge of the first "E" in the word "HEADLINE." By using gridlines, technical marketers can quickly create a number of different layouts that are balanced and organized.

Alignment, Balance, Flow, and Proximity

Alignment, balance, and flow guide consumers through chunks of content by influencing the direction they look as they scan technical marketing communication. The goal is to minimize wandering eyes, which can result in an overwhelmed or confused consumer. One way to achieve this goal is by creating an F or Z Pattern that places critical information in the top left corner of a design (as described previously). Another way to achieve this goal is through the design principle of proximity, which means grouping related elements near each other. According to this principle, elements that are placed closely together (that is, in close proximity of each other) appear to be related in some way. Conversely, elements that are pushed apart appear unrelated. When used effectively, proximity not only helps break content into chunks, but also enables consumers to quickly scan through those chunks in a way that helps them understand which elements are related and which are not.

For example, in the layouts shown in Figure 5.4, notice how consistent white space between elements creates a balanced grid that does not direct the consumer's eye in a specific direction. However, by increasing the white space of a vertical or a horizontal line, the technical

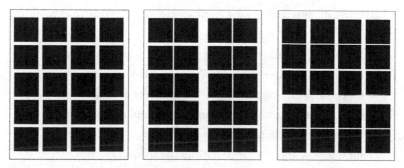

Figure 5.4 The use of white space in guiding consumer attention

marketer can influence whether a consumer views the page as columns or rows.

Keep in mind that too much white space as well as randomly placed graphics and text can make a layout feel top heavy, bottom heavy, or even chaotic (as if elements are fighting or simply floating and not part of the layout). All of these make engagement with the content more difficult and less enjoyable for the consumer.

Graphics

In addition to designing the layout, technical marketers must pay special attention to graphics, such as photos, charts, logos, and so on. The sections that follow provide insight into key roles that graphics perform in communicating technical marketing information.

Aesthetic versus Informative

One way to analyze and select appropriate graphics is considering whether they simply add to the beauty of a marketing piece or actually communicate information in a way that words alone cannot.

In the book *Visual Strategies*, researchers Felice Frankel and Angela DePace describe what they call "explanatory" graphics. By explanatory, they mean graphics that "can be used as evidence or proof."[8] Although Frankel and DePace focus specifically on graphics in science and engineering research, the concept of categorizing graphics by the roles they perform is valuable to technical marketers.

The categories of *aesthetic* and *informative* graphics are also helpful to marketers in considering how graphics are used in creative executions:

- Aesthetic graphics—This type of graphic adds to the visual appeal of a creative concept. For example, a marketing brochure promoting mortgage loans might include photographs of a couple smiling while signing paperwork with the loan originator. Although this type of photo might show a desk and the office setting, the main reasons for including the photograph would be to add visual interest to the brochure, instill a sense of happiness about the process, and direct the eye movement of the reader. In other words, such photographs are included to provide a pleasing experience for the audience, rather than knowledge or instructions.

- Informative graphics—This type of graphic is similar to Frankel and DePace's idea of a graphic that provides evidence. In other words, an informative graphic provides a visual fact or detail that the audience needs to understand a product or process as well as to make a purchasing decision. For example, the hypothetical mortgage brochure described previously may include charts or tables that demonstrate how low interest rates are now and what interest rates have been in the past. This information about rates might not only appear as a visual in the brochure, but would likely be combined with verbiage to explain the trend of rates to the audience.

What makes the informative graphic different from the aesthetic graphic is that it does provide facts or details that help communicate or clarify a marketing message. Missing out on that information would mean the audience would likely be less informed. Aesthetic graphics, on the other hand, simply provide visual appeal. As such, an aesthetic graphic can be overlooked without the risk of the audience being less informed.

It is important to note, however, that not all photographs are aesthetic. For example, a photograph displaying the effects of gum disease would certainly convey visual facts in a way that communicates (and clarifies) the importance of flossing and in a way that words alone cannot convey.

Icon, Index, and Symbol

Another way to categorize and select appropriate graphics is to focus on how the graphics relate to or represent the subject matter. Technical marketers can turn to semiotics for help with this approach.

Semiotics is the study of *signs* and how *meaning* is created. Although it is a complex subject with many aspects, technical marketers can focus on a couple of basic concepts. For example, according to Swiss linguist Ferdinand de Saussure, a *sign* is made up of two parts:

- Signifier—This is the word, image, or sound that is used in communication or thought.
- Signified—This is the concept that comes to mind when a person hears, sees, or thinks about the sign.

For example, after hearing the word *car* (which is a signifier), people often imagine a picture of a car (this image would be the signified concept). Of course, different people may imagine different pictures of cars. It may be a specific car, their own car, or a general silhouette shape of a car. The point, however, is that people would likely visualize an automobile with four wheels. Although the words *truck* and *SUV* would also conjure up visuals of automobiles with four wheels, those visuals would have a different size and shape in a person's mind than the visual of a car.

In another example, a visual featuring the silhouette of a cigarette with a line running diagonally through it would convey the message that smoking is not allowed. In that case, the silhouette of the signifier would be the cigarette silhouette, and the signified concept (or the meaning) would be the idea that smoking is not allowed.

The reason signs (as well as signifiers and signified concepts) are important is because technical marketers must always remember that consumers conjure up images and ideas when they come across words, images, or sounds. So a technical marketer must pay close attention to which words, images, and sounds are included in marketing materials—and whether they are conveying an accurate, effective message in the minds of the target audience.

When working on creative concepts for technical marketing communication, it helps to understand the different ways that a signifier (that is, a word, image, or sound) may be interpreted. Charles Sanders Peirce, who is considered the father of American semiotics, argued that signifiers can function as indexes, icons, and symbols. In the indexical mode, the signifier shares a direct connection with or indicates the signified. In the iconic mode, a signifier resembles a signified or has similar qualities.

In the symbolic mode, the relationship between the signifier and signified is conventional or habitual. These terms aid in understanding signifiers:

- Icon—An icon *resembles* something, which means the resemblance can be seen by another person. For example, the cigarette silhouette described above resembles the characteristics of a physical cigarette, and it displays those attributes in a way that people can see the similarity or resemblance between the silhouette and the physical object.

- Index—An index *indicates* something, which means that people can figure out the message by understanding the connection. For example, a smile indicates happiness, since people are usually happy when they smile. Smoke indicates fire, since smoke rises from fire. Similarly, a Mercedes Benz indicates wealth, since it is a luxury car and often only people with high salaries can afford to drive one. Therefore, when people see a smile, smoke, or a Mercedes Benz, they are able to figure out what those images indicate.

- Symbol—A symbol differs from the other two categories in that a symbol *must be learned.* Symbols neither resemble nor indicate. Instead, they are built on connections that have been established over time for a specific audience. For example, the color red does not resemble or indicate danger, and yet it is often used to communicate that message. However, in a different culture or context, the color red may indicate love or passion. The point is that symbols carry meanings that must be learned—and even then, different audiences or situations might impact how meanings are interpreted.

Although it is tempting to think of icons, indexes, and symbols as distinct types of signs, it is more accurate to say that a signifier may be an icon, a symbol, an index, or even a combination of all three.[9] For example, advertisements for a sports cars often show images of speedometers. As a meaning-making sign, the speedometer is indexical in that it is directly connected to the rotations of the wheels as an indication of speed. It is also iconic in its likeness or similar qualities, that is, in its display of numbers that depict roadside speed limit numbers (think about the connection between the number 55 on the speedometer and the 55-mile-per-hour speed limit in the 1980s). Finally, the speedometer is symbolic in the way it is perceived by drivers. In other words, the use of a needle moving up and down within a finite area creates a low, middle, and high perception in the mind of the driver.

Technical marketers must consider the different ways in which images may be understood by their audiences. That means that early in the creative process, time should be set aside to closely examine the elements (such as colors, images, and even word choices) that are included in the design. This may consist of describing what is included in the creative and what concepts the image is intended to convey. In that case, the technical marketer may not even use the terms signifier and signified, but would still be addressing those concepts when talking with the rest of the marketing team. That said, the discussion may also consist of an in-depth discussion of the index, icon, and symbol meanings—especially as they relate to the specific audience.

Regardless of whether a general or in-depth discussion is used, the discussed semiotic concepts can help technical marketers make purposeful decisions about what to include (and what not to include) in each marketing piece.

Choosing Graphics

Before placing a graphic in any marketing materials, decide which type of graphic will best convey the information:

- **Drawings**—Used to show objects or spatial relationships that are difficult to photograph or would be difficult to understand if photographed. For example, a watch can be shown in a drawing that removes unnecessary details or clutter. Such a drawing would also allow the technical marketer to simultaneously show the outside of the watch and the internal components by eliminating the face of the watch in part of the drawing (using techniques known as a cutaway or a cross-section).

- **Photographs**—Used to show objects and spatial relationships realistically. For example, "before and after" photographs convey a sense of reality that drawings would not be able to achieve.
- **Screen shots**—Used to show websites or applications that would appear on a computer, tablet, or smartphone screen. For example, a company may use a series of screen shots as part of its online ordering instructions.
- **Bar graphs**—Used to visually represent data, especially when comparing different categories. For example, when comparing the miles per gallon data of three different cars, a bar graph with three different bars may be used.
- **Picture graphs**—Used to visually represent quantities by showing recognizable, relevant images. For example, a graph showing the number of cars and trucks sold might use a silhouette of a car for the car quantities and a silhouette of a truck for the truck quantities. By doing so, the data are presented in a way that viewers can understand more quickly and easily.
- **Line graphs**—Used to show changes over time. For example, a line graph showing changes in mortgage rates over the past 30 years would help borrowers understand the trends over time and, as a result, make a decision about how good their current rate is in comparison.
- **Pie graphs**—Used to show how the parts make up a whole. This type of chart is only useful when the subject has a finite number or value. In other words, the parts must equal the whole when added together. For example, a pie chart may be used to show donors how a nonprofit company spends the money it raises.

continued

- **Flow charts**—Used to show relationships, such as the steps in a process. For example, an online ordering system may be explained by dividing the process into four different stages; each stage might be represented by a box with arrows leading from one box to the next.
- **Tables**—Used to organize and compare large amounts of data systematically. This type of graphic is especially useful when viewers want to compare all or only some categories. For example, a table can be used to compare mobile phone plans. In this case, the plans can be compared by categories such as cost, minutes, data, text messages, and so on. Viewers who are most interested in cost could focus on that category and easily compare all plans, while another viewer might choose to focus on the data comparison.
- **Maps**—Used to show geographic information, such as locations, boundaries, routes, distances, terrain, and so on. For example, a company may use a map to show customers where its store is located. Similarly, an airline company may use a map to show consumers the different routes and locations it offers.

Ethical Graphics

Technical marketers must also be aware of ethical misrepresentations and legal violations that can occur when using graphics.

One of the first concepts to consider is the source of the graphics. If the company (or one of its employees) did not create the graphic, the company does not own it. Marketing creatives must not use copyrighted graphics in whole or in part without prior permission from the owner (see the copyrighting section in Chapter 2 for more information). In other words, it is not acceptable (nor is it legal) to simply use a graphic from another source; just because an image is found on the Internet does not mean it is fair game. When permission to use a graphic is granted, the technical marketer must make sure the source is credited and that the terms of use are followed precisely. Even if the graphic is original to the company but is based on data from another source, that source must be credited in the marketing material.

In addition to following copyright laws and referencing guidelines when using graphics, technical marketers must be aware of the following:

- Clarity—Graphics must be easy to understand with just a quick glance. If too much information is presented in one graphic, divide the data into two or three graphics. If the lines or bars on a graphic are hard to differentiate, increase the contrast to help distinguish the information and avoid confusion. Review each graphic in detail and make sure that unnecessary clutter, colors, or callouts are removed. Make sure, however, that the necessary or purposeful colors or callouts are left in place to help convey the message.
- Misrepresentation—Technical markets must proceed with caution in an age in which computer software makes it easy to adjust charts, manipulate images, and add special effects. For example, changing the scale of a line graph (by either unnecessarily raising the scale or elevating the starting point) to minimize or emphasize data may be easy to do, but is misleading and unethical. So is cropping a photo to exclude important elements. Similarly, displaying a pie chart in three dimensions might seem like a convenient way to add interest, but it also distorts the perception of the chart in a way that may confuse and mislead viewers. Finally, focusing solely on inanimate objects (such as a broken piece of equipment in a warning sign) de-emphasizes human beings; to avoid such misrepresentation, technical marketers can include non-grotesque graphics of humans (such as generic photos, sketches, or silhouettes of people).[10]
- Integration—Graphics should not replace text, but should help explain the information. Therefore, technical marketers need to help clarify the relationship between the graphical and textual information. Effective integration of graphics can be achieved through *proximity* (placing the graphic near the text that it

relates to), *reference* (introducing and explaining the graphic in the text, such as telling readers how to interpret a graphic and directing them to "see the figure above"), and *captions* (short but informative text blocks under graphics to help readers understand the significance of a graphic and interpret its information).

By following these guidelines, technical marketers can rely on graphics to ethically convey information without confusing or misleading the audience.

Colors

A discussion of technical communication can hardly exaggerate the importance of color. It is not enough to merely acknowledge that color is everywhere; technical marketers must also consider how every piece of visual information is coded with color, and what meanings the coloring conveys. Change the color, and the message changes with it. That makes color a key element of every marketing message.

Notable Quote

"Anyone who claims to be an expert on color is a liar. A true expert would have to be fluent in physics, chemistry, astronomy, optics, neuroscience, geology, botany, zoology, human biology, linguistics, sociology, anthropology, art history, and cartography."[11]

—Joann Eckstut and Arielle Eckstut,
Color Consultants

Characteristics of Color

Typically, people describe colors by using common names: red, yellow, green, and so on. But anyone who has looked at a color wheel or peered into a box of crayons understands that there are multiple shades of reds and yellows and greens. Colors come in significant and slight variations. That means choosing (or even discussing) the right shade for a marketing campaign can quickly become confusing.

To speak more precisely about color, technical marketers should be familiar with three main characteristics of color: hue, saturation, and value.

Hue is simply another way to say color (thus the terms are synonyms). The six major hues are red, yellow, green, cyan, blue, and magenta. Of course, these are only the major categories; minor colors exist within the broad spectrum. For example, the color orange exists on a continuum somewhere between red and yellow.

Saturation is a way to discuss how vivid or dull a hue appears. A hue with 100 percent saturation is known as completely pure because no gray has been added. Such a color would appear rich. When gray is added to the hue, however, the shade becomes duller (and the saturation decreases). A helpful way to think of saturation is to imagine a gray film being laid over the color; the film would not appear to mix with the color, but would instead appear to cover it with a dull screen. So if technical communicators want to use a richer color, they would increase the saturation (thus, removing the gray impurities). Conversely, if a color was too rich or vivid, more gray could be added to the color (thereby decreasing the saturation level).

Finally, the value of a color refers to the brightness—or the amount of white or black mixed into the color. Unlike the gray used in saturation, the white and black colors do not appear as films that dull a color. Instead, white and black are mixed with the color to vary the shade lighter and darker. For example, on a scale of values for red, the higher values would appear pink and then completely white, while the lower values would appear burgundy before appearing completely black. For an easy demonstration of value, change the brightness on a computer monitor—sliding it one direction turns the screen completely white, and sliding it the other direction turns the screen completely black.

When combined together, the three characteristics distinguish one shade of color from another, which can save time and lead to more productive discussions when evaluating mockups of marketing materials.

Connotations of Colors

Although precise shades are important, technical marketers must also understand broad generalizations about the emotional connotations of each hue:

- Red is an intense and highly visible color, which is why it is often used in stop signs and emergency lighting. Depending

on the context, red may indicate desire, strength, and power;
however, it may also indicate anger, danger, bloodshed, and sin.

- Blue is associated with trustworthiness, dependability, and
  commitment, which makes it ideal for products and services
  related to cleanliness as well as the sky and water (such as
  ocean cruises, window cleaner, purified water, and so on).
  While blue suggests precision and tranquility, which can be
  useful when promoting complicated, high-tech products, it
  can also indicate depression and sorrow.

- Green is the color of nature. It can be used to symbolize
  growth, wealth, freshness, and fertility. Depending on the
  shade, green is associated with feelings of safety and harmony
  as well as with greed and sickness.

- Yellow can be used to gain audience attention quickly—
  especially when placed against black, which is why it is used
  for highway warning signs. Although yellow is associated
  with joy, happiness, and energy, it is also associated with
  childishness, cowardice, and spontaneity (which means yellow
  is not ideal for mature or sophisticated products and services
  but may work well for marketing children's products).

- Orange is less aggressive than red, but is still highly visible.
  In fact, orange is more visible than any other color when
  placed in front of blue (which explains why it is used for
  traffic cones and life rafts). Orange can be used to indicate
  happiness, creativity, determination, joy, endurance, and
  warmth but is also associated with flamboyance, tension,
  and stubbornness.

- Brown is the color of earth. Although it is often thought of
  as a dark, neutral color like black, it is more accurate to think
  of it as a duller shade of orange. It combines the sense of
  nature found in green with the reliability of blue. In addition,
  it is ideal for establishing a welcoming, pleasant marketing
  message. That said, brown may also convey cheapness or
  blandness.

- Pink carries some of the same energy of red, but in a softer,
  more sensual way. It is often associated with happiness,

passion, and romance, but can also been associated with feminine, soft, or gentle characteristics (which may not be appropriate for many products).

- Purple combines the dependability of blue with the intensity of red in a way that symbolizes royalty, luxury, and ambition. It can be used to convey wisdom, mysticism, and independence but can also convey arrogance. Generally speaking, purple appeals to creative or eccentric audiences; however, brighter shades of purple appeal to children.

- Black implies strength, authority, and formality. Depending on the product being marketed, black can help establish a sense of prestige or elegance as well as grief or fear. It can be used as a background color to make brighter colors standout but should be used with caution when displaying text, since light on dark text can decrease readability.

- White connotes cleanliness, purity, innocence, and goodness. When marketing health services or medical products, white can convey safety and sterility. Additionally, white adds a sense of ease and simplicity to technical products and services. Too much white, however, can be seen as empty, incomplete, or isolating.

Did You Know?

- **Colorless**—Light waves are colorless until they are processed by the brain. Photoreceptors in the eyes actually sense the light's wavelengths, and then the brain associates colors with each sensation. In other words, grass is not really green and a stop sign is not red. Instead, they are sensations that we experience and interpret as color.

- **Primary Colors**—Primary colors are not as primary as people think. When talking about mixing paint, the

continued

primary colors are red, yellow, and blue. Those colors are considered primary because they cannot be created by mixing other colors. But, when talking about mixing light waves, the primary colors are red, green, and blue (RGB). These three colors can be used to create every other color when their light waves are mixed (which is how computer monitors display color).

- **Black and White**—A white computer screen is the result of RGB all being lit equally at their maximum intensity. A black computer screen, however, is created by the absence of all colors.

Fonts

Perhaps the most common act of designing is placing text on the page or screen. Technical marketers must choose what size the text should be and what mood it should convey. They also must factor in readability and placement. All of these aspects must be addressed in the font choices.

To accomplish this task, page designers must first read and understand the text. Too many designers treat the text as just another element to be dropped into a page design. That is a mistake. Designers must understand the message, including what is being said, to whom, why it is being said, how the reader might feel about it, and the desired outcomes for both the company and the consumer. Once these questions are answered, the designer is ready to select a font that conveys the appropriate tone.

Notable Quote

"Letters are microscopic works of art.…When the type is poorly chosen, what the words say linguistically and what the letters imply visually are disharmonious, dishonest, out of tune."[12]

—Robert Bringhurst,
Typographer and Book Designer

Selecting Fonts

When choosing fonts, consider the following characteristics:

- Typeface—The typeface refers to the specific name of a font. Some common typefaces include Helvetica, Arial, and Times New Roman. Each typeface has a specific look. For example, **Arial** has a thin, streamlined appearance, whereas `Courier` has a classic typewriter appearance. Making sure that the typeface's appearance matches the tone of the subject matter is an important part of page design. Another important factor is whether to choose a serif or sans serif font. Serif fonts (such as **Times New Roman**) look more decorative, with small lines extending from the edges of the letters. These small lines can help connect the letters and make text easier to read. Based on that, serif fonts are often used for longer passages of text or more official documents (such as reports or spec sheets). Sans serif fonts (such as Arial), on the other hand, are cleaner fonts because they lack the small lines. Sans serif fonts are often used for shorter text, such as headlines, subheads, captions, callouts, and so on. That said, sans serif fonts are commonly used for web text as well as more casual or creative pieces, such as magazines or advertising copy. Be careful, however, not to use too many different typefaces in the same marketing piece. Instead, select a few typefaces that look good when used together but are also different enough to help readers distinguish between a headline and the body copy.
- Size—Font sizes are measured in points. To put point sizes into perspective, just remember that 72 points equal one inch. Most professional documents will use 9- to 11-point text for the body copy. Headlines and subheads would be larger (perhaps 28 to 48 points), while captions or footnotes would be smaller (around 6 to 8 points). Despite these suggestions, it is important to remember there are not any rules for font sizes. The three main goals are to (1) choose font sizes that are readable for the audience, (2) use contrasting sizes to establish

hierarchy, and (3) use consistent sizes for similar elements, such as using the same font size for all subheads.

- Styles and effects—Style characteristics include bold, italics, or even both bold and italics at the same time. Effects, on the other hand, include underlining, all caps, small caps, superscripts, subscripts, and striking through text with a line. These characteristics can be applied to any typeface to help make specific words stand out or to convey unique messages. For example, technical marketers may bold a product name to help make it more prominent. A superscript number or asterisk, however, would indicate that the reader should look at the footnote that follows for more information. These characteristics should be used sparingly and for specific purposes; overuse makes the text hard to read and reduces the reader's ability to locate important information.

Formatting Text

After selecting the appropriate typefaces, sizes, styles, and effects to be used, the technical marketer must focus on shaping how the text appears in the layout. Some of the most common ways to shape text are to adjust the following:

- Vertical spacing (the space above and below each line of text)—The amount of space between lines is called *leading* (which is pronounced like *threading*). Although most people are familiar with the terms *double spacing* and *single spacing*, leading is actually based on points (just like font sizes).

  Text with lines that are too close or too far apart can be difficult to read. To avoid this problem, the leading should be at least one if not two points higher than the font size. For example, text written in an 11-point font should have at least 12 or 13 points leading. Sometimes the leading can be adjusted to eliminate a *widow* (i.e., a word or single line of text that cannot fit on the same page or in the same column as the rest of its paragraph and, therefore, appears at the top of the next page or column). When working with subheads, remember to focus on the principle of proximity (items that are closer appear to be related). Based on this principle, the space above the subhead should be greater than the space below it; that way, readers associate the subhead with the text that follows it.

- Horizontal spacing (the space to the left and right of words or letters)—Adjusting the spacing between all of the words in a line of text is called *line spacing* or *tracking*. This spacing is helpful when trying to eliminate an *orphan* (i.e., a single word that appears on a line all by itself at the bottom of a paragraph). Sometimes, however, a designer will only want to adjust the spacing between two letters—especially in headlines or large callouts where the letter spacing will be more noticeable. This type of adjustment is called *kerning*. Kerning is often used sparingly for specific letter combinations. For example, when the letter "w" is followed by the letter "e," a designer may want to tuck the "e" closer to the empty space in the bottom half of the "w." The opposite can also be true; two letters may need to be pushed apart. For example, a designer may need to separate the letter "f" and the letter "i" since the top of the "f" may fall too close to the dot of the "i."

In addition to spacing, line lengths should be considered when designing text. Long lines of text become burdensome and harder to follow, while short lines of text can seem choppy or disjointed. So it is good idea to keep the line lengths to approximately 8 to 14 words per line. This length can be achieved by dividing the space into two or even three columns of text.

Finally, the alignment of the text can impact the readability of marketing communication. Broadly speaking, technical marketers have four types of alignment from which to choose (see Table 5.1).

Using these techniques to format the text will make the text more reader friendly and will more effectively integrate the promotional copy into the overall layout. The result is more understandable and aesthetically pleasing technical marketing messages.

Table 5.1 Four types of text alignment

Type of alignment	Characteristics	When to use
Left aligned	Lines of text are aligned on the left side of the paragraph NOTE: To identify the beginning of a new paragraph, the first line of text can be indented slightly or a blank line can be added before the paragraph	Left aligned is the most commonly used type of alignment for body copy because it is easy to read (and requires very little adjustment by the designer)
Right aligned	Lines of text are aligned on the right, which creates a ragged left margin. The ragged left margin is harder to read, since the audience does not have a consistent left line to return their eyes to as they read down the page	Right-aligned text should be used sparingly and for specific types of text (such as callouts or sidebars)
Centered	Lines of text are centered horizontally on the page, which creates ragged left and right margins. When used for long text, this type of alignment can seem chaotic and confusing	Centered text should be used only for concise lines or phrases (such as headings or short quotes), not multiple paragraphs of text
Full justified	Lines of text are aligned on both the left and right margins, which creates a well-defined text area. This type of alignment is harder to read because odd spaces appear between words and slow down readers	Full justified text is often used for text-heavy manuscripts, such as novels or some magazines. That said, only experienced designers who are skilled in adjusting the spacing of text should attempt this type of alignment

Chapter Summary

The chapter has explained how to design effective technical marketing communication by:

- Using presence and gestalt psychology to influence audience perceptions
- Applying contrast, repetition, alignment, and proximity to achieve balance, flow, and emphasis

- Choosing graphics that will accurately and ethically convey visual information
- Making appropriate color choices based on common characteristics and connotations
- Understanding key aspects of font selection—including typefaces, sizes, and formatting.

The next chapter focuses on aspects of technical marketing communication that are unique to different delivery options.

Recommended Resources

Technical marketers who want to learn more about design principles should consider the following books:

- *The Non-Designer's Design Book, Fourth Edition* (Robin Williams. San Francisco: Peachpit Press, 2015), which is ideal for technical marketers who are new to design.
- *Document Design* (Miles Kimball and Ann Hawkins. Boston: Bedford/St. Martin's, 2008), which covers a wide variety of design topics that are ideal for mid-level designers and technical marketers.
- *Elements of Graphic Design, Second Edition* (Alex White. New York: Allworth Press, 2011), which explores in-depth design concepts that can inspire even expert designers and technical marketers.

Endnotes

1. Perelman, C., and L. Olbrechts-Tyteca. 1971. *The New Rhetoric: A Treatise on Argumentation.* Notre Dame, IN: University of Notre Dame Press.
2. Tucker, R.E. 2001. "Figure, Ground and Presence: A Phenomenology of Meaning in Rhetoric." *Quarterly Journal of Speech*, 87, pp. 396–414.
3. Perelman, C. 1982. *The Realm of Rhetoric.* Notre Dame, IN: University of Notre Dame Press, p. 36.

4. Kauffman, C., and D.W. Parson. 1990. "Metaphor and Presence in Argument." In *Argumentation Theory and Rhetoric of Assent*, eds. D.C. Williams and M.D. Hazen. Tuscaloosa, AL: University of Alabama Press, pp. 91–102.

5. Koffka, K. 1935. *Principles of Gestalt Psychology*. New York, NY: Harcourt, Brace and Company.

6. Köhler, W. 1929. *Gestalt Psychology.* New York, NY: Liveright, p. 149.

7. Hedberg, M. 2003. *Mitch All Together.* Compact Disc. Produced by Jack Vaughn. New York, NY: Comedy Central Records.

8. Frankel, F., and A.H. DePace. 2012. *Visual Strategies: A Practical Guide to Graphics for Scientists and Engineers*. New Haven, CT: Yale University Press, p. 13.

9. Chandler, D. 2002. *Semiotics: The Basics*. New York, NY: Routledge.

10. Dragga, S., and D. Voss. 2001. "Cruel Pies: The Inhumanity of Technical Illustrations." *Technical Communication*, 48, no. 3, pp. 265–274.

11. Eckstut, J., and A. Eckstut. 2013. *The Secret Language of Color: Science, Nature, History, Culture, Beauty of Red, Orange, Yellow, Green, Blue and Violet*. New York, NY: Black Dog and Leventhal, p. 8.

12. Bringhurst, R. 2005. *The Elements of Typographic Style*. 3rd ed. Vancouver, BC: Hartley & Marks, p. 23.

PART III

Delivering Technical Marketing Communication

CHAPTER 6

Delivery

After focusing on writing and design in the previous two chapters, this chapter provides overviews of how to deliver technical marketing communication using common media. Specifically, this chapter describes:

- Website marketing
- Social media marketing
- E-mail delivery
- Blogging for business
- Traditional print media

Checklists are also provided.

Website Marketing

Today, the Internet is home to more than 1 billion unique website host names. While this number ebbs and flows, the sheer volume of online competitors who are only a mouse click or finger tap away is staggering. The online landscape is further complicated by the swift judgments consumers make about a website and the organization responsible for it and how long they choose to engage with both. To put it directly, today's consumers want to get in, find what they are looking for, and get out quickly.

A number of factors should be considered when designing a website so that the site serves its intended purpose, is easy to navigate, and is inclusive.

Usability, User-Centered Design, and User Experience

Usability is concerned with how individuals use web technology to complete specific tasks in an efficient, effective, and satisfactory manner. The study of user-centered design and the user experience provides insights into web users' understanding, expectations, and comfort level with web technology as well as their behavior patterns when using technology.

Information gained from usability studies helps assure that web design is consistent, familiar, easy to learn, and reliable. While aesthetic design of a website influences the overall first impression of a website and the organization responsible for that site, a visually appealing site does not necessarily make a site more usable. If consumers cannot get into a website and find what they are looking for, they will leave and find another resource that is easier to use.

Ideally, consumers (and not just employees of an organization) should be involved in the web design process, from initial concepting through iterative design stages and final testing. Involving consumers early on helps ensure a website is functional, well designed, and appropriately labeled. Only through direct contact with likely users, will web development teams gain full understanding of familiarity with word choices, typical navigation patterns, clarity of directions, data security concerns, and so much more.

Accessibility and Inclusive Design

Ensuring accessible, inclusive website design is a legal requirement under the Rehabilitation Act of 1973 for any organization that receives federal funding, including government offices, private and public corporations, and educational institutions from elementary school through college. Regardless of funding, the practice of providing accessible, inclusive design is the right thing to do.

Accessible, inclusive website design considers how individuals with varying physical or cognitive abilities engage with a website. The World Wide Web Consortium has developed Web Content Accessibility Guidelines (WCAG) for building and rendering web pages to make them accessible to everyone.[1] Design guidelines address the use of color and minimum contrast thresholds and the ability for consumers to increase font size for readability. WCAG also addresses the use of speak-aloud content, such as the use of *alt tags* to describe graphics and the use of hard-coded H1 and H2 headings that are read aloud when consumers are using a screen reader to navigate a page. The guidelines also address the use of captions with multimedia and the inclusion of multiple formats that allow consumers to see or hear content is explained. Other detailed functions allow users to navigate a website fully using keyboard commands only.

For a complete discussion of how to make a website accessible and inclusive, search online for *WCAG* or *Web Content Accessibility Guidelines* from the World Wide Web Consortium. Several online tools also are available to check websites for accessibility. Some tools address a specific accessibility guideline, such as color contrast. Other tools will do a thorough page check and provide an explanation of what elements are not compliant.[2]

Analytics

Analytics are a valuable resource to better understand effectiveness of web design and content as well as how consumers engage with a specific site. Web analytics can be used to determine what words consumers are using to search in a website, which pages are being visited most frequently, how long consumers spend on each page, and much more.

Website Checklist

Content:
- ✓ Relevant to the primary audience of the website. Why would they come to the website, and what do they need in order to complete a task or take the next step?

Text:
- ✓ Page title/URL that uses keywords
- ✓ Navigation labels that are familiar to the consumer
- ✓ Clear, concise headlines and subheadings that use keywords
- ✓ Topic stated within the first couple of sentences using keywords and clear, concise language

continued

✓ Short paragraphs that use keywords and clear, concise language (approx. three to six sentences per paragraph)

✓ Links to relevant events, news articles, product web pages, social media sites, and so on

✓ Specific call to action

Images:

✓ Royalty free with the source attributed (or purchased for the specific usage)

✓ Relevant to the topic

✓ Concise caption to explain the image or connect the image to the text

✓ Brief description of the image included in the "Alt Text"

Design:

✓ Key information in F reading pattern hot spots

✓ WCAG accessibility guidelines are met

Social Media Marketing

The biggest challenge in understanding social media and its role in marketing is that new social media services are continually popping up. Some have staying power, while others might not. Rather than just jumping on the latest trend, the trick is to compare the different options available and how they can be used to further the objectives of the organization (see Table 6.1).

Regardless of which social media services are chosen by an organization, two guidelines should be followed:

- Provide consistent, meaningful content—Social media content should be frequent (strive for daily) and something the target audience cares about. While many companies like to use social media to promote special offers, most social media followers are looking for content that will make their lives better and more enriched. Create an editorial calendar that plans for time-sensitive content, feel-good content, and content that

Table 6.1 Comparison of three social media services

Social media service	Mission	Type of service	Types of connection
Facebook	To give people the power to share and make the world more open and connected	Social network	Communicate stories, videos, images, and ideas that engage and excite people. The look, feel, and tone are conversational and personal
LinkedIn	To connect the world's professionals to make them more productive and successful	Professional network	Establish professional expertise, make valuable connections, share industry news, and professional development
Twitter	To empower everyone to create and share ideas and information instantly without barriers	Micro-blog	Share ideas in 140 characters or less, follow ideas and individuals, and establish expertise

showcases expertise. Built-in social media analytics will indicate the type of content that resonates positively with consumers.

- Invite engagement—Social media sites are about connection and engagement. If an organization is only posting one-sided content and not inviting engagement, the relationship is not rewarding. It is like going on a date and the other person only talks about himself or herself. Comment on or share posts from others, tag people and businesses, and invite others to engage with content posted by asking questions. All of these actions will grow a stronger social media network and expand marketing reach.

Big-box retailer Walmart provides an example of how an organization might use different social media platforms for technical marketing. Walmart has web pages devoted to tips and ideas for living well at learn.walmart.com. These pages house blogs, videos, and other resources to teach consumers ways to add healthier foods and habits to their daily routine. On Facebook, Walmart then offers healthy recipes that can be created in minutes using only a few, inexpensive ingredients. The company also provides short how-to videos from fitness experts on how—in as few as 10 minutes each day—consumers can easily form life-changing habits. These Facebook posts link the user directly to the healthy-living web pages for more information. Twitter posts are also used to direct followers to the web pages with posts, such as:

"Exercise #Just10 mins-Visit Americas Biggest Health Fair 10/10 12-4pm @ ur local @Walmart http://bit.ly/1OjHzkW #ad"

On LinkedIn, Walmart shares its corporate philosophy, challenges, and successes of initiatives through media stories, infographics, presentation videos, and more.

Three Types of Social Media Posts

To generate content for social media posts, consider using the following types of posts:

- **Time-sensitive content:** Current events, key deadlines, and limited time promotions
- **Insightful help content:** "Did you know?" posts, tidbits, and "Top 3 Tips" to accomplish a task
- **Feel-good content:** Success stories, employee profiles, seasonal/holiday traditions, and fun facts

Hashtags

On social media, hashtags are keywords or phrases preceded by the pound or number symbol "#." A hashtag must be written as a single word, without any spaces. While it can include numbers, punctuation and special characters would not work. Hashtags allow social media users to follow ideas or themes simply by searching the hashtag and being directed to a feed of all posts that include the same hashtag. In the previous example, "#Just10" was the hashtag used to unify all posts in the Walmart campaign.

Character Counts

Each social media service has specifications for posting content, such as what resources can be shared and how many characters can be included in a post (see Table 6.2).

Table 6.2 Comparison of content specifications for three social media services

Posts at a glance	Facebook	LinkedIn	Twitter
Character limit, including spaces	63,000+ characters	700 characters	140 characters
Photo sharing	Yes	Yes	Yes
Video sharing	Yes	Yes	Yes
Built-in URL shortener	No	Yes	Yes

Social Media Checklist

Topic:
- ✓ Relevant to the company's products/mission as well as a subject the target audience cares about

Text:
- ✓ Concise and attention-getting
- ✓ Within character count limits of each social media service
- ✓ Links to relevant events, news articles, blog posts, product web pages, and so on
- ✓ Relevant hashtags if part of a larger, ongoing theme or idea
- ✓ Interactive with reader comments and questions

Image(s) and videos:
- ✓ Royalty free with the source attributed (or purchased for the specific usage)
- ✓ Relevant to the topic

Technical marketers must consider how their content will fit within particular social media service specifications. For example, URL links are often included in posts, but long URLs can result in the content exceeding the character limits of a service. Using an online URL shortener, such as Bitly or TinyURL, will help. Both LinkedIn and Twitter have automatic URL shorteners that create smaller URLs in a random mix of characters. Other URL shorteners allow some customization.

Blogging for Business

A blog (which derives from the words *web log*) is a website or web page that enables regular sharing of information or ideas around a particular topic. This sharing is done through short posts written in a conversational tone at regular intervals, such as three times weekly. Blogs provide an opportunity to showcase expertise, expand marketing reach with prospects, and build brand recognition. To build readerships, each blog post should be promoted on social media with a link to the blog. E-mail signature blocks should also include a link to the blog.

The Word on Word Count

When it comes to blogs, a well-written post of 150 words can engage and excite the target audience as effectively as a 1,500-word post. The key is to understand the audience and the content they care about. Longer blogs typically are how-to posts or researched based with links to data and other resources. Certainly it is important to vary blog post length for variety, but adhering to a hard-and-fast rule about word count is not necessary (unless, of course, a blog is predicated on this, such as "Financial news in 500 words or less").

Calls to Action

Expanding marketing reach is a primary goal of blogging. This would not happen without specific, purposeful calls to action. Common blog calls to action to expand reach include variations of the following:

- Follow us on social media
- Get our daily blog delivered to your inbox
- Sign up to receive our monthly newsletter
- Share this post on social media
- E-mail this to a friend

Typically, these calls to action are in multiple locations, such as at the end of each post as well as in sidebars.

Other calls to action are often embedded in the copy of the blog or in a sidebar. For example, if readers can download a free ebook to learn more, that might be highlighted in a sidebar. To further reinforce credibility and engagement, a post might direct readers to previously published blogs by saying "read more or see related posts" and then providing links to other blog post titles.

Make it Easy to Engage

If a call to action encourages people to share content with others, make it easy for them to do so. Include social media sharing buttons. Ensure that forms to opt in to RSS feeds and e-newsletters are available to help deliver content automatically in multiple formats. Most blogging platforms already have this functionality built in, and bloggers simply need to check a box to activate each feature.

Blog Checklist

Topic:

  ✓ Relevant to the company's products or the blog's mission

Text:

  ✓ Concise, attention-getting headline

  ✓ Topic stated within the first couple of sentences

  ✓ Subheads to help divide long text into smaller sections

  ✓ Short paragraphs (approx. three to six sentences per paragraph)

  ✓ Links to relevant events, news articles, previous posts, product web pages, and so on

continued

✓ Invitation for readers to interact with the post's ideas (such as asking questions)

✓ Call to action that keeps readers connected to your content and invites more readership

Image(s):

✓ Royalty free with the source attributed (or purchased for the specific usage)

✓ Relevant to the topic

✓ Concise caption to explain the image or connect the image to the text

✓ Brief description of the image included in the "Alt Text"

E-mail Delivery

E-mail marketing is great for generating qualified leads and converting these leads to sales. Among other things, e-mail is efficient in its automation capabilities, affordable, and instantly measures effectiveness (or lack thereof). While the writing and design strategies described in this book directly apply to e-mail marketing, the medium itself has additional nuances that must be considered to maximize e-mail efforts.

Subject Lines

One key to standing out in a cluttered inbox is to ensure e-mail subject lines are compelling, capture attention, and encourage consumers to open e-mails. In addition to the writing strategies shared in Chapter 4, marketers must write e-mail subject lines that are 55 characters or less, including spaces (less than 45 characters is ideal). And, the most important words should appear first. Why? Inbox configurations on mobile devices and desktop computers only show so many words; the rest are cut off. Keeping subject lines concise ensures consumers see the complete message.

Content Integration

Calls to action in e-mail should take consumers to another trackable activity, such as downloading a free ebook, scheduling an online demonstration, reading a blog, signing up for a monthly e-newsletter, or getting a free sample. In most cases, e-mails should link consumers to an online form that asks for additional contact information and preferences. If the call to action is to download a free ebook, have an opt-in box to also receive an e-newsletter. When consumers complete these actions, they move from being a prospect to being a qualified lead who wants to learn more about the organization, product, or service. This does not mean they are ready for a sale; however, it does indicate they are interested in staying connected. And that ongoing connection will hopefully lead to a sales conversion. Moreover, when consumers receive ongoing content they care about, they are more receptive to hard sales pitches.

Testing and Analytics

The beauty of e-mail marketing—compared to traditional print—is the immediate analytics that are available. Within minutes, marketers can see how e-mails perform: how many people opened an e-mail, clicked through an e-mail, and completed the call to action.

More importantly, analytics allow marketers to easily test the performance of e-mail content and delivery based on changes to one variable (called split testing or A/B testing). Marketers can test one subject line against another by keeping all the content the same, including the call to action, formatting, and delivery date and time. Marketers can test the format of an e-mail, using text-only e-mails compared to designed HTML e-mails. Again, the content, subject line, delivery date, and time would all be the same; only the e-mail format would change. Marketers can test calls to action or design elements such as placement of a graphic or color of a headline. Finally, marketers can test send times or days, sending the exact same e-mail at the exact same time on a Tuesday and on a Thursday or sending the exact same e-mail on a Wednesday but one at 9 a.m. and one at 3 p.m. Effective split testing only tests one variable; changing multiple variables will not provide meaningful feedback.

SPAM Check

In its basic sense, SPAM is any single e-mail that is sent in bulk to a large audience. While some e-mails may be legitimate marketing e-mails, plenty are sent by misguided individuals with bad intentions. To minimize risk of viruses, harmful schemes, and loss of productivity, many organizations have implemented security measures to reduce delivery of junk e-mail or e-mail from unknown senders.

Marketers should take steps to maximize delivery of e-mail campaigns by understanding current standards for monitoring SPAM. One useful step is to use one of several free SPAM checkers available online to analyze the content of e-mails for anything that could be flagged. Organizations also can improve deliverability by using e-mail addresses from individuals who opted into marketing/communications via an online form. Additionally, e-mails can have a callout that reminds consumers to mark the sender as an approved sender.

Because technology is always changing—and hackers are always looking for clever ways to make everyone's life more difficult—marketers should stay on top of current trends in SPAM and standards in antivirus protection.

Legal Requirements (that Bear Repeating)

As noted in Chapter 2, commercial e-mails are subject to federal requirements defined in the CAN-SPAM Act of 2003. This law sets the rules for commercial message content, gives recipients the right to have organizations stop e-mailing them, and spells out tough penalties for violations. One requirement is that the sender of the e-mail must provide the ability for consumers to opt-out or unsubscribe from the organization's marketing/communication messages. The law explicitly states that organizations must honor the request within 10 business days. Complete requirements of this law can be found on the Federal Trade Commission website.

E-mail Checklist

Topic:
  ✓ Single topic focus relevant to prospects or qualified leads

Text:
  ✓ Concise, attention-getting subject line in 55 characters or less
  ✓ Topic stated within the first couple of sentences

✓ Subheads to divide long text into smaller sections

✓ Short paragraphs (approx. three to six sentences per paragraph)

✓ Specific call to action that links to contact information form for ongoing communication

Image(s):

- Royalty free with the source attributed (or purchased for the specific usage)
- Relevant to the topic
- Concise caption to explain the image or connect the image to the text
- Brief description of the image included in the "Alt Text"

Functionality:

- Marketing integration set up properly
- SPAM check used to assure CAN-SPAM compliance
- Prominent or consistent placement of unsubscribe or opt-out link

Traditional Print Media

Traditional print marketing is a broad category that involves a wide variety of marketing approaches. The following sections discuss traditional media that are commonly used to convey technical marketing communication.

Print Advertisements

Print ads appear in a variety of sources, including magazines and newspapers. They can be used to promote sales, reinforce past purchases, build brand identity, and even reassure investors or employees.

Although they may differ in the size, use of color, and print quality, most print ads share similar characteristics:

- Each ad focuses on a specific feature or point, with broader campaigns used to deliver multiple ads that emphasize various points.

- Print ads have a focal point. Sometimes a headline is prominently displayed near the top of the ad to gain the reader's attention. Other times, however, an image will dominate the ad.
- Print ads typically feature short copy (the exception would be pharmaceutical ads, which might be described more accurately as public information, rather than promotion).

Mail Order Materials (Catalogs and Direct Mail)

Even in today's age of technology, mail order materials are an important method of marketing. In some instances, mailings can reach consumers who cannot be reached through technology. In other instances, mailings can target specific individuals (such as potential customers who have expressed interest in a product) to provide detailed, customized information.

Targeted mail order materials might consist of a direct mail package, which would include a sales letter, print collateral (such as brochures and specification sheets), a special offer, and an order form related to a specific product or family of products. For a less targeted, specific approach, technical marketers often mail catalogs to past and potential customers. The catalogs are typically designed to look like a magazine in terms of size and paper type. However, catalogs provide very little text copy—opting instead to provide short descriptions and images of numerous products. Like the direct mail package, the catalog would include an order form as well as special offers. Although mail order materials are printed, they typically include calls to action that help drive customers to the phone and online ordering for ease and convenience.

Brochures and Spec Sheets

Brochures and spec sheets are used to provide an overview of a product or service. Based on their size and inexpensive production costs, they can be used in numerous ways (e.g., in mailings or as leave-behind collateral). While brochures are typically written with a feature-benefit approach, spec sheets focus more on technical characteristics, performance statistics, product components, and other factual information.

Although brochures and spec sheets can both include graphics, brochures tend to feature a balance of aesthetic and informative graphics, whereas spec sheets often rely on informative (highly technical) graphics. In terms of writing styles, brochures convey information using paragraphs with some bullet lists; conversely, spec sheets rely significantly on concise phrases.

White Papers

White papers are subtle (or soft-sell) marketing materials. Rather than directly promote the features and benefits, they focus on a business problem. Typically, white papers are formatted to look like reports, with a cover page, table of contents, specific sections related to the problem or industry change, and back matter (such as a bibliography or appendix).

The report format is actually what makes white papers appealing to potential clients. Rather than feel as if they are being sold a product or service, potential clients feel as if the company is reporting useful information about a problem or need clients face. The marketing information is then subtly presented as a way to solve the problem.

Newsletters

Newsletters are like short newspapers that are published by an organization. Like white papers, newsletters are a subtle form of marketing. Often they include feel-good stories, company updates, fun facts or quotes, and community-building tidbits (such as birth announcements or recipes). They can be delivered in print or electronic form (such as a PDF that can be downloaded from an organization's website or as an e-mail).

The top of the first page should display a banner that includes the newsletter's name, date, volume/issue, and the organization's name and logo. A table of contents should also be included in a prominent place to help readers navigate the newsletter quickly. Articles should be written using an inverted pyramid approach, which places the most important information at the top of the article.

Finally, depending on how newsletters are distributed, they must be compliant with the CAN-SPAM Act of 2003. Among other things, this means recipients must have the ability to opt-out or unsubscribe. Additional information about this law can be found in Chapter 2 and on the Federal Trade Commission website.

Traditional Media Checklist

Print advertisements:
- ✓ Attention-getting focal point (image or headline)
- ✓ Z Pattern layout
- ✓ Feature-benefit approach

Mail order materials:
- ✓ Catalogs feature product images and short descriptions
- ✓ Direct mail features sales letter and print collateral (e.g., a brochure)
- ✓ Special offer
- ✓ Feature-benefit approach
- ✓ Order form

Brochures and spec sheets:
- ✓ Brochures use feature-benefit approach
- ✓ Spec sheets focus on lists of technical characteristics, statistics, and components
- ✓ Relevant to the topic

White papers:
- ✓ Report format (including citation of sources)
- ✓ Information about a relevant problem, change, or opportunity
- ✓ Product or service subtly marketed as a solution to the problem

Newsletters:
- ✓ Subtle marketing
- ✓ Inverted pyramid approach
- ✓ Banner with newsletter name, date, volume/issue, and organization's name and logo
- ✓ Table of contents
- ✓ SPAM check and CAN-SPAM compliance, if e-mailing

Chapter Summary

The information in this chapter extended the concepts of writing and design to specific delivery options and provided checklists that technical marketers can use to develop:

- Legal and accessible marketing websites and e-mail campaigns.
- Social media posts and corporate blogs that actually engage with audiences.
- Traditional print materials that extend online marketing efforts.

Although this chapter highlighted the unique aspects of those marketing options, it is not intended to stand on its own. Rather, it should be read and applied with all the chapters that came before it. Thus, the information in Part I of this book connects with Part II, which (in turn) can be applied to Part III.

In the end, technical marketing communication is a complex, multifaceted activity. Only through comprehensive analysis and purposeful application can today's technical marketers achieve success.

Recommended Resource

Technical marketers who want to learn more about marketing media should consider:

- *Fundamentals of Writing for Marketing and Public Relations* (Janet Mizrahi. New York: Business Expert Press, 2010)

Endnotes

1. World Wide Web Consortium. (2015). "Web Design and Applications." Retrieved from http://www.w3.org/standards/webdesign (November 14, 2015).

2. Readers interested in learning more about these online resources can visit the following sites: Web Content Accessibility Guidelines by the Worldwide Web Consortium (http://www.w3.org/TR/WCAG20), WAVE Web Accessibility Evaluation Tool by WebAIM (http://wave.webaim.org), and Color Contrast Checker by WebAIM (http://webaim.org/resources/contrastchecker).

Bibliography

Anderson, R. E., & Jolson, M. A. (1985). Technical wording in advertising: Implications for market segmentation. In L. K. Moore & D. L. Plung (Eds.), *Marketing technical ideas and products successfully* (pp. 244–253). New York, NY: IEEE P.

Aristotle. (1984). *The rhetoric and the poetics of Aristotle* (W. R. Roberts & I. Bywater, Trans.). New York, NY: The Modern Library.

Bly, R. W. (2007). *The copywriter's handbook: A step-by-step guide to writing copy that sells*. New York, NY: Macmillan.

Bringhurst, R. (2005). *The elements of typographic style* (3rd ed.). Vancouver, British Columbia, Canada: Hartley & Marks.

Chandler, D. (2002). *Semiotics: The basics*. New York, NY: Routledge.

Cialdini, R., & Schultz, W. (2004). *Understanding and motivating energy conservation via social norms*. Menlo Park, CA: William and Flora Hewlett Foundation.

Dobrin, D. N. (2004). What's technical about technical writing. In J. Johnson-Eilola & S. A. Selber (Eds.), *Central works in technical communication* (pp. 107–123). New York, NY: Oxford University Press.

Dombrowski, P. (2000). *Ethics in technical communication*. Needham Heights, MA: Allyn and Bacon.

Dragga, S., & Voss, D. (2001). Cruel pies: The inhumanity of technical illustrations. *Technical Communication, 48*(3), 265–274.

Durack, K. T. (2004). Gender, technology, and the history of technical communication. In J. Johnson-Eilola & S. A. Selber (Eds.), *Central works in technical communication* (pp. 35–43). New York, NY: Oxford University Press.

Eckstut, J., & Eckstut, A. (2013). *The secret language of color: Science, nature, history, culture, beauty of red, orange, yellow, green, blue & violet*. New York, NY: Black Dog & Leventhal.

Fetscherin, M., & Usunier, J. C. (2012). Corporate branding: An interdisciplinary literature review. *European Journal of Marketing, 46*(5), 733–753.

Frankel, F., & DePace, A. H. (2012). *Visual strategies: A practical guide to graphics for scientists and engineers*. New Haven, CT: Yale University Press.

Gudema, L. (2014, November). 7 marketing technologies every company must use. *Harvard Business Review*. Retrieved from https://hbr.org/2014/11/7-marketing-technologies-every-company-must-use. January 31, 2016

Harner, S. W., & Zimmerman, T. G. (2002). *Technical marketing communication*. New York, NY: Longman.

Hedberg, M. (2003). *Mitch all together* [Compact disc]. Jack Vaughn (Producer). New York, NY: Comedy Central Records.

Herrington, T. A. (2003). *A legal primer for the digital age*. New York, NY: Pearson.

Henson, L. (1996). Why and how to advance technical copywriting. *Journal of Technical Writing and Communication, 26*(2), 193–209.

Goldstein, N. J., Cialdini, R. B., & Griskevicius, V. (2008). A room with a viewpoint: Using social norms to motivate environmental conservation in hotels. *Journal of Consumer Research, 35*(3), 472–482.

Kauffman, C., & Parson, D. W. (1990). Metaphor and presence in argument. In D. C. Williams & M. D. Hazen (Eds.), *Argumentation theory and rhetoric of assent* (pp. 91–102). Tuscaloosa: University of Alabama Press.

Koffka, K. (1935). *Principles of Gestalt psychology*. New York, NY: Harcourt, Brace.

Köhler, W. (1929). *Gestalt psychology*. New York, NY: Liveright.

Levine, J. (1996, December 16). Brands with feeling. *Forbes*, pp. 292–294.

Lewis, H. G. (1984). *Direct mail copy that sells!* Englewood Cliffs, NJ: Prentice-Hall.

MacInnis, D. J., & Stayman, D. M. (1993). Focal and emotional integration: Constructs, measures, and preliminary evidence. *Journal of Advertising, 22*(4), 51–66.

McAlhone, B., & Stuart, D. (1996). *A smile in the mind: Witty thinking in graphic design*. London, UK: Phaidon.

Mainwaring, S. (2011). *We first: How brands and consumers use social media to build a better world*. New York, NY: Macmillan.

Mesthene, E. (2003). The social impact of technological change. In R. C. Scharff & V. Dusek (Eds.), *Philosophy of technology: The technological condition*. Malden, MA: Blackwell.

Perelman, C. (1982). *The realm of rhetoric*. Notre Dame, IN: University of Notre Dame Press.

Perelman, C., & Olbrechts-Tyteca, L. (1971). *The new rhetoric: A Treatise on argumentation*. Notre Dame, IN: University of Notre Dame Press.

Prince, G. (1974). *A grammar of stories*. The Hague, Netherland: Mouton.

Rohne, C. F. (1985). Technical communication in marketing. In L. K. Moore & D. L. Plung (Eds.), *Marketing technical ideas and products successfully* (pp. 234–239). New York, NY: IEEE P.

Stewart, M. (2002). *Launching the imagination*. New York, NY: McGraw-Hill.

Sullivan, L. (2012). *Hey, Whipple, squeeze this: The classic guide to creating great ads*. Hoboken, NJ: John Wiley.

Sussman, L. (1999, July–August). How to frame a message: The art of persuasion and negotiations. *Business Horizons*, 2–6.

Teich, T. (2005, December). Marketing communication and technical communication: Not so strange bedfellows. *Intercom*, 9.

Torres, A., Bijmolt, T. H., Tribó, J. A., & Verhoef, P. (2012). Generating global brand equity through corporate social responsibility to key stakeholders. *International Journal of Research in Marketing, 29*(1), 13–24.

Tucker, R. E. (2001). Figure, ground and presence: A phenomenology of meaning in rhetoric. *Quarterly Journal of Speech, 87*(4), 396–414.

Walzer, A. E. (1989). The ethics of false implicature in technical and professional writing courses. *Journal of Technical Writing and Communication, 19*(2), 149–160.

Wiebe, G. D. (1951). Merchandising commodities and citizenship on television. *Public Opinion Quarterly, 15*(4), 679–691.

World Wide Web Consortium. (2015, November 14). Web design and applications. Retrieved from http://www.w3.org/standards/webdesign

Index

OTHER TITLES IN OUR CORPORATE COMMUNICATION COLLECTION

Debbie DuFrene, Stephen F. Austin State University, *Editor*

- *SPeak Performance: Using the Power of Metaphors to Communicate Vision, Motivate People, and Lead Your Organization to Success* by Jim Walz
- *Today's Business Communication: A How-To Guide for the Modern Professional* by Jason L. Snyder and Robert Forbus
- *Leadership Talk: A Discourse Approach to Leader Emergence* by Robyn Walker and Yolanta Aritz
- *Communication Beyond Boundaries* by Payal Mehra
- *Managerial Communication* by Reginald L. Bell and Jeanette S. Martin
- *Writing for the Workplace: Business Communication for Professionals* by Janet Mizrahi
- *Get Along, Get It Done, Get Ahead: Interpersonal Communication in the Diverse Workplace* by Geraldine E. Hynes
- *Managing Virtual Teams, Second Edition* by Debbie D. DuFrene and Carol M. Lehman
- *The Language of Success: The Confidence and Ability to Say What You Mean and Mean What You Say in Business and Life* by Kim Wilkerson and Alan Weiss
- *Writing Online: A Guide To Effective Digital Communication at Work* by Erika Darics
- *Writing For Public Relations: A Practical Guide for Professionals* by Janet Mizrahi

Announcing the Business Expert Press Digital Library

Concise e-books business students need for classroom and research

This book can also be purchased in an e-book collection by your library as

- a one-time purchase,
- that is owned forever,
- allows for simultaneous readers,
- has no restrictions on printing, and
- can be downloaded as PDFs from within the library community.

Our digital library collections are a great solution to beat the rising cost of textbooks. E-books can be loaded into their course management systems or onto students' e-book readers. The **Business Expert Press** digital libraries are very affordable, with no obligation to buy in future years. For more information, please visit **www.businessexpertpress.com/librarians**. To set up a trial in the United States, please email **sales@businessexpertpress.com**

CPSIA information can be obtained
at www.ICGtesting.com
Printed in the USA
FSOW03n2309250617
35616FS